Presentation of Prophecy

Second Edition

COLETTE TOACH

www.ami-bookshop.com

Presentation of Prophecy
Second Edition

ISBN-10: 1626640726
ISBN-13: 978-1-62664-072-6

Copyright © 2016 by Apostolic Movement International, LLC
All rights reserved
5663 Balboa Ave #416,
San Diego,
California 92111,
United States of America

1st Printing May 2014
2nd Edition May 2016

Published by **Apostolic Movement International, LLC**
E-mail Address: admin@ami-bookshop.com
Web Address: www.ami-bookshop.com

All rights reserved under International Copyright Law.
Contents may not be reproduced in whole or in part in any form without the express written consent of the publisher.

Unless specified, all Scripture references taken from the New King James Version®. Copyright © 1982 by Thomas Nelson. Used by permission. All rights reserved.

Contents

Contents 3
Chapter 01 – How to Prophesy 8
   The Truth About Prophecy 9
   Prophecy – Step 1 and 2 12
   Breaking Prophecy Down 14
   Prophecy and Faith 16
Chapter 02 – What to Do if God Does Not Speak 20
   General vs. Personal Prophecy 23
Chapter 03 – How to Judge Any Revelation 30
   INTRODUCTION – Discovering a Foreign Land… 30
   As a Prophet You Sometimes Feel Like Being in a Foreign Land 31
   There Are Two Ways to Judge Revelation 31
   Three Different Voices 32
   Stop Thinking So Much 36
   Knowledge Does Not Equal Revelation 36
   Stupid Clay Vessel? That's Me! 37
   Your Control Tower 37
   The Voice of the Enemy 38
   The Voice of the Lord 44
   Identifying the Three Voices 49
Chapter 04 – Common Mistakes of Prophecy Presentation 52

- Enlighten Believers 54
- Effects of Wrong Presentation 55
- Be Sensitive to the Spirit 65
- Revelation on Demand 66
- Charging for Words 67
- Prophesying Your Own Burdens 68
- Not Word-Based 70

Chapter 05 – Getting Prophecy Presentation Right! 74
- Effects of Correct Presentation 74
- Revelation of Jesus 74
- Opened Church's Eyes 76
- Explosion of Word and Spirit 77
- Psalmody, Praise and Worship 78
- Words of Wisdom 80
- Inner Healing 80
- True Faith 82

Chapter 06 – The Image of Prophetic Ministry 86
- Wrong Presbyteries 86
- Correct Presbytery 95

Chapter 07 – Dos & Don'ts of Prophetic Presentation 102
- Don'ts of Presenting Prophecy 102
- Dos of Presenting Prophecy 113

Chapter 08 – Ministering to Others 126

Introduction – Learning When to Step Forward & When Back 126

God's Perfect Timing 127

Learn to Be Sensitive to the Spirit 129

The Revelation is Not Necessarily Wrong – It's Just the Timing.. 133

Wait for the Body of Christ to Be Ready 135

So... When is the Time to Get Involved? 137

Don't Pounce on People... 138

What Are You Going to Do? GET INVOLVED! 140

Chapter 09 – Master Other-Orientation 144

Listen to the Hints 144

Master the Skill.. 146

Three Steps for Ministering to Others..................... 148

The Other-Orientation Project 150

About the Author 152

Recommendations by the Author 154

I'm Not Crazy - I'm a Prophet 154

Practical Prophetic Ministry 155

Prophetic Essentials 155

Prophetic Functions 156

Prophetic Anointing 156

A.M.I. Prophetic School... 157

Contact Information 158

CHAPTER 01

How to Prophesy

Chapter 01 – How to Prophesy

1 Thessalonians 5:20 Do not despise prophecies.

I had the wonderful opportunity once to go on a hot air balloon. I had a friend whose parents did it as a sideline business. Over weekends they would take people up for a champagne breakfast. It was very popular with honeymooners.

After tagging along over weekends for some time, we were allowed to go in a ride of our own.

I wasn't quite sure what I was expecting - perhaps a big rush - but it was really different to what I thought it would be.

One of the first things I realized when we were going up is that I felt as if I was standing on air. It was the most amazing thing. Even though I had the basket around me, I didn't feel afraid or insecure - I felt safe.

The other thing that I didn't realize (even though it is quite logical when you think about it) is that when in a hot air balloon, you can't dictate which direction you want to go in. You are at the mercy of the wind.

You hold the power to get in the basket and turn on the burners. Once you are in the air though, that's it. You are at the mercy of the wind.

The way this couple did it, is that one person would be in charge of the balloon and the other would follow it on the road with the truck, so that wherever they landed they could meet up.

When it comes to speaking out a prophetic word it is much like a hot air balloon ride.

You chose to get up in the air, but once you are there it is up to the wind, which could blow you in any direction.

All you can do is get in the basket, fire up the burners, get into the air and wait for the wind to blow. Then enjoy the ride, because the rest is up to the Holy Spirit.

The Truth About Prophecy

It is a lovely illustration of a prophetic word because it is a perfect picture of you and the Lord working together. There is your part and there is the Lord's part. Your part is very simple. You just need to come to a place of making yourself available.

Then it is up to Him to blow the wind. If He doesn't blow it, you are not going anywhere. If He does blow it, you are going in His direction.

You are out of control and that is a scary place to be for some people, but it is the best place to be for a prophet. There is nothing better than having the Lord in control.

You Are not the Wind

There are times the wind just doesn't blow. You step up to the plate and make yourself available, but nothing happens. God decides to go on vacation and leave you holding the baby.

So there you stand in the middle of the field, nicely suspended in the air all ready to go… but going nowhere fast. What do you do?

It is such a common trend amongst some ministries to just step out, open your mouth and prophesy whatever comes out or to just prophesy and prophesy until something comes.

That would be like me standing under the hot air balloon, taking a deep breath and trying to use my own strength to create a wind, waiting for something to happen.

Listen… you are not the source of the wind. You are just the vessel.

The wind comes from the Holy Spirit. It is for Him to blow and for you to just make yourself available.

You got it a bit mixed up here. You cannot say, "Let's jump in there and give the prophetic word and hope that somewhere along the line the anointing suddenly kicks in."

By God's grace, sometimes it does and you breathe a sigh of relief. If you keep pushing on that way though you are just pushing on with your mind and what comes out is going to come out as a load of garbage, and a load of logic and understanding.

Using Prophecy Correctly

By the end of this chapter you will have the wisdom you need to flow in prophecy correctly. You will learn that being effective does not mean standing up and prophesying the first thing that comes to your head!

I have seen the most ridiculous things in the prophetic ministry. I have heard some prophets say to someone needing ministry, "What profession are you in?"

"I am a bricklayer."

"Well, just as you are a bricklayer in the natural so the Lord is calling you to lay bricks for the Church of God and …"

Are you serious? That is like standing under the balloon and blowing the wind yourself.

Here is a little tip… let God blow the wind. You get in the basket and fire up the burners, then leave the rest up to the Lord!

You are already pumped up by speaking in tongues, you already have a face-to-face relationship with the Lord Jesus – now it is just a case of, "Lord, here I am. I make myself available to you."

When it comes to speaking out a prophetic word this is not a time for you to make things up. When you are journaling you have the liberty to mess things up.

When you are busy practicing at home and you are feeling your way around, it is okay to make things up a bit to get yourself going.

If you mess it up while in your prayer closet it is just you that has to suffer. When it comes to prophesying over other people you don't have that luxury of making things up – because it is their lives in the balance now.

Prophecy – Step 1 and 2

What happens if you make yourself available and nothing happens? That is why I want to give you some tips and hints here of how to deal with it. I also want to help you to become confident in speaking out prophetic words – so let's get to it then!

Step 1. Make Yourself Available

Making yourself available is like getting in the basket. It means putting yourself in a place to be used of the Lord.

It means deliberately putting yourself in a place to be used of Him. If there is a need you are the first to ask the Lord, "Do you want me to say something Lord?"

So many think that God will throw them over His shoulder and dump them into the basket, forcing them to participate. Remember, the Lord Jesus is a gentleman, He is not going to drag you through the streets by your hair like a caveman!

He will wait for you to put yourself in place. Make yourself available. Ask Him to use you and once you do that the revelation will flow.

You will see a vision, receive the first words to a prophecy or hear something in the spirit.

Step 2. Open Your Mouth

It is only when you open your mouth though that you fire up the gas, light it and you slowly ascend into the air.

Until you open your mouth and speak out what God gives you, you won't receive any further direction. Opening your mouth is like turning on the burner.

Then as you start to ascend, the wind is going to blow and your prophetic word will change direction.

Perhaps you are in a public meeting or in personal ministry and somebody needs direction from the Lord. You make yourself available by saying, "Lord, here I am. I am available."

In that moment you might get a vision. Perhaps you will just get a few words, "I am with you…" That's all you get.

It's very seldom that the Lord, gives you a full sentence when it comes to prophecy. He gives you the first few words or perhaps just an impression in your spirit.

As you are praying you sense that the road that the person is going down or the direction they are taking is wrong. The Lord doesn't clarify or show you anything else – just that one piece.

This is Where Faith Counts!

What are you supposed to do with that? Well, then open your mouth. Until you open your mouth, you are not going anywhere. If you are sitting and waiting for the full revelation and picture, then let me break the news to you... it is not coming!

You have to step out in faith and say, "Thus smith the Lord, the part of the road that you are going down right now is going to lead you into destruction, but I have something better for you..."

The direction will come, the revelation will come, and the wind will begin to blow and you will start feeling a flow.

Breaking Prophecy Down

There are some simple guidelines to follow when prophesying. So in true form, I will break it down nicely for you, so that you are never left without the "know how" ever again!

Get Yourself in the Basket

So there you are in a ministry situation and you have made yourself available to the Lord.

You get an impression in your spirit. Perhaps you see a winding road in the spirit - a difficult road. When you see it, you know, "Ah, that's what the word is about." Or perhaps you hear the words, "The road has been difficult..."

That's all you get! Well, you are only going to fire up those burners when you open your mouth and you speak those first words. When you are new at it you may fumble a bit (actually even when you are comfortable with it, you still fumble sometimes).

I think that the Lord allows us to mess up every so often just to keep us humble!

That's when you fire up the burner and then you will sense the flow of the spirit and the words will keep coming but then suddenly it will stop...

Don't "Ride" the Anointing

That's the part where you shut up. I know, some prophets get so excited that God is using them, that when God stops blowing the wind, they carry on pushing with their own little bits that they always wanted to tell the pastor.

They cannot help but try to get in the juicy parts that he was not willing to listen to before. They try to ride the anointing.

You try to ride the anointing to get in everything that has been on your mind.

No adding your own bits to prophecy! When the revelation stops then you stop.

Get out of the basket. The ride is over. Finished!

Prophecy and Faith

Our walk is one of faith. It is one of God reaching down to man and not man reaching out to God. It is what makes our Christian walk, even as believers, different from every other religion out there.

Our religion is based on the fact that while we were yet sinners He gave us His grace.

Your prophetic walk is based on the fact that while you were the most pathetic, useless loser God could find, He called you.

Your calling depends on His ability to speak to you and not your ability to hear His voice.

It is not your ability to hear God's voice that makes you a prophet. It is God's ability to speak to you and to raise you up with a prophetic anointing that makes you a prophet.

Every believer should be able to hear God's voice because He is speaking to us all the time.

When it comes to ministry and to giving a prophetic word, it is for God to speak. That's why He is God. He is the originator. You are not the originator. Have you got my point yet?

Giving God Control of Prophecy

There are times when God will not speak. He is God... He is allowed to do that.

It is not for you to say, "God, I need a prophetic word, everybody is looking at me."

Who are you? You are just a clay pot. If the master doesn't want to pour wine in you and pour you out again... You know what? It is for the master to decide.

Sometimes we forget that. We get so full of the grace of the Lord and the fact that He will always just be there that we forget that He is a very sovereign and righteous God who has a will of His own.

When He wills, He does what He wants and it is not for you to push the hand of God and force Him to speak when He does not wish to speak.

He is a very holy God. One that should be held in fear and respect as much as to be held in love and adoration. Until you have that fear and respect for our heavenly Father you are going to give the wrong impression to the body of Christ.

When you have that godly fear and respect for the Lord and you do speak a prophetic word you are really going to speak it on His behalf, because you will know that it is coming from the Throne Room - it is not coming from your mind. You are not just another prophet spouting the first thing that comes to your head.

Have the Courage to be Different

Be different! Stop comparing yourself with all the others that are prophesying.

It reminds me of Elisha in 2 Kings 3 again when all the other prophets were prophesying, "Go forth, you will be victorious..."

They were giving their big fanciful prophetic words and Elisha is the only one who has the courage to say, "Actually, the Lord says that you will not win this battle. Instead, you will be slain and you will not survive this day."

Guess, whose word came to pass? The prophets who spoke the first thing that came to their heads or the one that spoke from the Throne Room of God?

Which one are you going to be? What is more important to you? To speak the truth or to have everybody say, "Well, he is such a mighty prophet, he can just prophesy anytime he wants?"

No, you can't prophesy any time you want. You prophesy when God speaks. If God doesn't speak it might feel uncomfortable but it is what will separate you from a prophetic "wannabe" and a true prophet of God.

CHAPTER 02

What to Do if God Does Not Speak

Chapter 02 – What to Do if God Does Not Speak

I know how uncomfortable it is to stand in a meeting or be faced with someone with an urgent need, only for God to grow ominously silent!

So let me give you a few lessons I learned myself along this process. Hopefully as you apply these points, you will feel more confident and also have the courage to only speak when you get a revelation.

All is not lost though if God grows quiet. There is a way to save face and still look like you know what you are doing! The prophet faces enough humiliation in his lifetime without having to look like he has "lost it" in the middle of a meeting.

So gather around and take some notes, because you never have to feel lost ever again!

1. Speak in Tongues

The first thing you can do is speak in tongues - especially when you are in personal ministry.

If you bring the situation to the Lord and He does not answer simply speak in tongues and let your spirit pray to God, until you feel a release.

That is a wonderful way to say, "Okay Lord, it is in your hands. Your will be done."

Maybe the person you are ministering to isn't ready for the revelation yet. Maybe it is not time. Let God be in control of the direction that the balloon goes in.

2. Release Blessing

The next thing that you can do is to speak blessing. As a believer you have the authority to speak blessing in the name of Jesus.

The Lord has given us the authority in this earth just as He gave it to Adam to speak things into existence, to speak blessing and to speak His will according to the Word.

Say for example that you have somebody that has come to you with a marital problem. It could be a wife that feels that their husband is having an affair. Perhaps it is a husband struggling with something their wife is doing.

You bring the situation to prayer and… you get nothing.

You are thinking, "Lord, what do I do here?" As a prophet and as a believer you can lay your hands and speak blessing.

You can say, "Lord, you know the care that my brother or sister is facing right now and I just speak your blessing on this situation.

I know that according to your Word that marriage is of you and so I stand against the enemy on behalf of my brother and I pray that you will bring your hand now and bring reconciliation."

You might not have received a "Thus saith the Lord" but you can certainly pray according to the word He has already given us in the Scriptures!

3. Stand on the Word

Say for example that somebody comes to you with a physical or spiritual need. The Lord does not show you a thing! No vision, no prophetic word... never mind no wind, you do not even get a gentle breeze!

What now? The Word is clear and it stands true. You can speak peace on their situation. You can do as Jesus did and speak to the winds and the waves, "Peace, be still!"

Somebody comes to you with a financial problem. They keep having problem after problem and they don't know what is going on. They need revelation and you get no revelation. This does not mean that you cannot minister to them in love.

You can say, "Lord, I know it is not your will for your children to suffer. Lord, the Word says that you will meet our needs according to your riches in glory. You are a giver of good gifts.

I speak blessing on the finances. I speak prosperity that everything their hand touches will prosper, just as you said in the Word."

Do you see the importance of all the bulldozing that I taught about in the Prophetic Essentials book? So even if you don't get revelation it doesn't mean you can't pray. You can pray the prayer of faith just like it instructs us to do in:

> *James 5:15 And the prayer of faith will save the sick, and the Lord will raise him up. And if he has committed sins, he will be forgiven.*

General vs. Personal Prophecy

There is a lot of confusion on the difference between personal and general prophecy. So once again, pick up your notebook and write down some points.

I promise this will bring such a release in the way you minister. Sometimes just knowing the "what, when and how" of these two prophecy types, how to deliver them falls into place easily.

The General Prophecy

> *Acts 15:32 Now Judas and Silas, themselves being prophets also, exhorted and strengthened the brethren with many words.*

General prophecies are fun and they are given to a group. I say that they are fun because they inspire everybody! The reality is that hardly anyone remembers them, but that is okay. The people leave the meeting feeling, "Yes, I heard from God".

They are the kind of words described in this scripture above.

General prophecies are given to a group of believers.

They can have a few messages in them, but they relate to more than one person. If you are in a public meeting this is the kind of prophetic word that you can receive.

General Prophecies Are Motivational

Another characteristic of a general word is that it is usually motivational. As a group the Lord will say, "You are going in the right direction. I know that you are going through a tough time right now, but I am there for you and I am going to hold onto you. I am going to get you through it."

They are the kind of words that you need to hear straight from the Lord. Words like, "I am there for you. Hang in there."

Never stop giving those, because they uplift the body of Christ. They give faith, hope and love.

General prophecies are there to help us go for a little while longer. You just need to hear the Lord say every now in a while, "Hang in there. I am not going to let you go. I am there to help you through. Don't get discouraged."

That is not to say that a general prophecy cannot also issue a warning or be directional. The Lord might also be saying to a group, "Don't allow the enemy to put bitterness in your heart. Let it go."

You need that quick conviction every so often! We need it just like we need some tasty ice-cream every now and again on a hot summer's day just to feel good.

We need that good stuff. It makes our life worth living. Sure, you cannot base your life on it, but it is those sweet moments that give you what you need to press on through.

Personal Prophecy

> *2 Samuel 12:7 Then Nathan said to David, You are the man! Thus says the Lord God of Israel: I anointed you king over Israel, and I delivered you from the hand of Saul,*

Now on the other side we have personal prophecy. What makes this different is that as personal prophecy is a word given specifically to an individual – just like in the word we see here that Nathan gave to David.

Very often it is quite personal, that is why it is called "a personal prophecy!" It is personal to them. It will touch on things that they might want to keep hidden or on things that are hurtful.

Nathan did not walk through the streets of Israel and declare this word and what would happen – he had a private audience with David.

You don't stand up in the middle of a crowd and say, "Thus saith the Lord, your marriage is in trouble."

"You are living in sin!"

"God is going to bring you to death."

"You have hurt from an abuse of the past that God wants to heal!"

There are just some things that do not need to be broadcasted over the entire congregation!

Let's raise up prophets who have the courage to give the personal prophecy to the person it is intended for.

Change the Trend!

Let's change the trends a little. There have been times when God has led me to single somebody out in a public meeting and say, "Rise up. Don't allow the enemy to steal God's blessing from you."

However, more often than not, I share a word like that in a private setting, after the meeting. If that is not possible the Lord arranges circumstances where I can minister to them personally.

No More "Drive by" Prophecies

To me, when I give somebody a personal prophecy it is a very specific message for them and I like to follow it up afterwards. If the Lord gives somebody a direction through a prophetic word, I like to follow it up with practical ministry.

If the Lord says that He is going to release them into prophetic training, I like to follow that up and say, "The Lord is releasing you as a prophet. This is what you are going to go through. These are the next steps that you are going to have to take now."

Perhaps you give a personal word and the Lord says that He is going to bless their business or that the road they are on is blocked and He needs them to take a new direction.

When I am finished giving that word I want to give them some counsel in that direction. I want to tell them the "what, why and where".

Multiple times a day we get people writing in or contacting us saying, "It was prophesied over me that I am a prophet, but I don't know what to do now." They were just hit with a "drive-by" prophesy!

Let's stop the "drive–by prophesying" shall we? Do not rattle off your prophetic word and then run out of the door.

Do you know how many times prophets in the Old Testament prophesied over the kings and the leaders? After each word they gave it was always followed with counsel and advice.

They delivered their word and then they said, "The Lord says that you must follow through with this action..."

When Samuel anointed Saul as king, he shared the prophetic word, but then he told him what he needed to do and what was going to happen afterwards. He did not just leave it at that.

From all the examples in the Word, you can see that the personal prophecy can range from being a warning, encouragement or even a word of judgment. That is why it is vital to share it with the appropriate person.

Becoming Comfortable With Prophecy

I know that it may be time effective to just call people out in the middle of meetings, but how much of an effect are you really having? So many leave the meeting thinking, "I was not good enough for the Lord. He had something to say to everyone except for me."

That is why I am a keen advocate of the general prophecy. When you make it a habit to share a general prophecy, everyone leaves that meeting feeling as if they heard from the Lord. It helps them know that God does not play favorites.

Get your categories straight. If the Lord has given you a prophetic word for an individual, share it with them privately. Give them the opportunity to save face. Do not expose their dirty laundry in front of everyone.

You will humiliate them and close any doors for real ministry. On the other hand, if you get a general prophecy, do not be afraid to share it in the group setting. Everyone will be able to revel in the anointing.

At the end of the day, it is our role to bring maturity to the Church through a relationship with Jesus. So motivate publically and prophecy personally in private. It will set you apart not only as a prophet, but as a leader others are keen to receive from.

CHAPTER 03

How to Judge Any Revelation

Chapter 03 – How to Judge Any Revelation

INTRODUCTION – Discovering a Foreign Land…

You have not experienced traffic until you have sat in the border crossing between Tijuana - San Ysidro and San Diego for two hours.

It is unlike anything you have ever seen. You sit behind row after row of cars and it is bumper to bumper as far as the eye can see.

These are some of the experiences we had when we first came to Mexico… border traffic as well as the huge traffic circle that is right in the middle of Tijuana - cars don't drive there but they aim…

Fortunately, when we first arrived we had family who had already been here and so they could show us around town a bit. That way we could feel a little bit familiar in this extremely foreign land.

It took us a while to realize that there are times when it is good to go to town while at other times it is best to stay at home. Having been here a few years now we can judge when the traffic will be difficult and when it will be more easy-going.

We now know where everything is and so when somebody else comes to visit, we are the ones that can show them around. We can show them the places that are good to visit and the places that are not so good. We also know where to get the best and most traditional tacos in town.

As a Prophet You Sometimes Feel Like Being in a Foreign Land

So what has this got to do with receiving and judging revelation? Well, as a prophet sometimes you feel like you are being thrust into a world that is very different and foreign to you, especially if you have only just discovered your prophetic calling.

It can be a little scary at times. Especially as you start receiving revelation and you are not sure where to go from there. You think that you are taking a good direction but you end up in a traffic jam or in a bumper to bumper bashing with somebody else and wonder what you are doing wrong!

There Are Two Ways to Judge Revelation

How can you learn to judge revelation? Well, there are two ways. The first way is to arrive in a foreign land, pull out a map and try to figure out the best way. It will take you longer but it can be done.

The other way is to have somebody who is familiar with the territory show you around. Well, that is what this chapter is all about and what I am here for.

I want to show you around a little bit and help you see how to receive and judge revelation. I want to help you understand when to speak, when not to speak and discern what's of God and what is not.

I give you a more detailed and comprehensive teaching on how to judge revelation correctly in my book *Practical Prophetic Ministry*. However, there are three points that I don't cover in detail there and so I want to cover them here.

These three points are not only important but are a matter of confusion as you start getting going in your walk.

You get revelation but sometimes you wonder if it was really God or just you. Sometimes you might even wonder if you are in deception.

Three Different Voices

In short, there are three different voices you can hear in your heart. Sometimes, it's the Lord who is speaking, other times it can be the enemy and then it could also be "you" speaking to you - in other words, the voice of your mind.

How do you discern between these three voices? How do you know what's God, how do you know what's your mind and what's the enemy?

Well, I am here to help you with that and show you the best route to go. Hopefully you will be able to go through your prophetic training without getting into hot water and without making too many mistakes.

On second thought though, being a prophet goes hand in hand with making mistakes. It comes with the territory. Regardless of that, I am hoping that you can reduce the level of the mistakes you make.

The Voice of Your Mind

So, let's jump right in and let's take a look at what the voice of your mind sounds like. How do you know if a revelation that you are receiving is really of the Lord or if it's just you coming up with some fancy ideas?

I would say that the most outstanding principle is that your mind is logical. This sounds obvious, doesn't it? Think about it for a while though. Your mind is logical. It is going to think according to what you know, according to what you've read and according to the thoughts you have in your mind.

1. Your Mind is Logical

So if you are getting a revelation that is logical and you say to yourself, "Oh yeah, I expected God to say that! It makes sense...!" When you feel that way, I would be a little cautious of that word, hold back a bit and wait for some confirmation.

Why? When God speaks, it is called revelation because it is something that was revealed to you that you didn't know before.

You might have a sense in your spirit that God wants to do something or an impression of perhaps where things are going. However, when God gives a revelation even though it seems obvious when you get it, it's new and fresh. It is something you didn't consider and didn't think of before.

And so when you are working along and suddenly you get this very logical idea and you think, "Oh yes, that's exactly what should happen and where we should go", I would hold off on that for a bit!

2. What You Want to Hear

Your mind likes to play tricks on you and it will be logical and that's why it's best to wait when you sense something like this. Your mind will tell you what you like to think and what you want to know.

So if you are in prayer and you get a revelation that seems logical, I am not saying it's entirely not of the Lord, I am just saying that it probably needs to be worked through a little bit. That is why it is so important to have people around you who can be there as a confirmation.

If you don't have anybody that you can pray or share with, know that we are always there for you. You can just drop us a line or sign up in our prophetic school.

There is no better way to learn than to ask. There is no better way to get it right, than to discover your mistakes and your shortcomings first.

How to Judge Any Revelation

You see, if you can see where you are messing up - then you will also know it when you get it right.

There is no better confidence booster than "knowing that you know" that this word is of God and that you are saying it with authority. It gives you such a faith booster to have this kind of confidence. Then when you speak with that kind of faith, the word comes out with such power.

3. Not Every "Revelation" is From God

So don't be afraid to sift through the revelations and don't be so naïve and arrogant to think that every revelation you get is of God!

That would be really naïve because your mind often works over time. Especially when you get too analytical and think about everything from what God should do, what you want Him to do, to what this person should do. Then when you get a revelation you try and fit it into all that.

Also, realize that you are not a teacher! You are a prophet. You will hear me say that to you many times. I am not saying that prophets are stupid, dumb bunnies who walk around and don't know anything.

Rather I am saying that your reliance is not on your mind but on your spirit and the revelation God gives you. The only thing you should be feeding into your mind is the Word of God! When you do that you can be sure that the revelation that is coming up is of Him!

Stop Thinking So Much

So let's put away the analyzing and let's stop trying to figure things out. By the time you get to prophetic office you will be ready to study a bit more but for now you really have to put your mind aside and quiet those thoughts.

You have to quiet those arguments in your head, put them on the cross and let God take control. This is one of the greatest hindrances. If you are battling to flow in any of the spiritual gifts or are battling to move forward in your calling right now, I can guarantee that one of the main problems is right up in your head. You think too much… stop it!

Knowledge Does Not Equal Revelation

We get so many folks that contact us and are only interested in what degrees and certificates they can get from our courses. You know, we do offer that. If you want that and want to learn we are there to give you knowledge.

However, a prophet with just a bunch of knowledge is not a prophet at all. It is not about the things he knows but it is about the things he does and the things that God tells him.

With a teacher this is different. What he knows is very important and knowledge is a main factor in the teaching calling.

Sure, let's not be ignorant either. That is even what the Scripture says, let's not be tossed around by every wind of doctrine. Let's know the Word of God.

However, let's just face the reality guys! Our strength doesn't lie here and thank you Lord Jesus for that! This is no intellectual competition! It is what God has put in your heart and the fire He has given you.

Stupid Clay Vessel? That's Me!

Stop trying to act and look intelligent and just be the stupid clay vessel! Let me tell you a secret... When you do that, you will have a lot more fun!

You will start enjoying life, because those revelations are going to bubble up from deep within.

I am not saying, "Don't think." I am saying just don't think so hard all the time but give God a chance to speak. Give that analytical mind of yours a rest.

Put aside the arguments and the "yes... buts" the "why Lords" and the "how comes?"

Let the Holy Spirit speak to you from your spirit and I promise you - He will start answering your questions before you have a chance to even ask them.

Your Control Tower

When God speaks to us, that word comes from our spirit into our soul which is then expressed in our body through our words and actions. Your soul is like your control tower and that is where your mind sits.

So what happens if God is trying to speak, but you are up there in your control tower busy trying to figure things out all by yourself?

Well, guess what? The revelation can't get through. You are so hung up on your mind that you have blocked your spirit off.

Instead you need to look in the Word, let God speak and then think about it afterwards. However, give the poor guy a chance to speak from time to time, okay?

The Voice of the Enemy

Now how do you know when a revelation is directly from the enemy? For this I can give you some very clear pictures.

1. Forceful Revelation

The first thing is that it will be really forceful.

You could be going about your business and the next thing you know is you get this, "You have to drop everything now and you have to go and tell that person this word!"

This is not the voice of the Lord. The Lord is gentle. He is the epitome of the English gentleman. He leads you by the hand, opens the door and moves the chair for you…

That is the picture of the Lord Jesus. He isn't going to slap you on the face, pick you up, run out of the door with you and shout, "Speak to this person here!"

He doesn't say, "Stop right here at the side of the road and jump up to grab that person and tell them about me!" That is not the Lord and it is not how He operates!

The more you come into that intimate relationship with Jesus the more you will understand this concept. He is not forceful! He doesn't "jump you".

When you see somebody operating in this way, let me tell you, that is not the voice of the Lord!

"You must do this now or you will be cursed!"

No, that is not the voice of the Lord Jesus. Did you ever hear Him say that to His disciples? Did He ever say to them, "You better go out now, two by two or I will curse you!"?

No, He sent them with a promise and said that He would be with them and they would move in signs and wonders. They wanted to go. In fact, He couldn't hold them back from going!

2. The Word Brings Fear

The voice of the Lord doesn't bring fear. Let's say you were in a meeting and you didn't bring the prophetic word and you think, "Oh, I had the word but didn't bring it. Their blood is on my hands! I failed the Lord", and now you are full of fear and guilt.

That is not the Lord at all. It is probably just as well you didn't open your mouth to speak because it may have been a deception.

The enemy will certainly try to come at you with that voice many times. He will play on your mind, push you and come at you from without.

That is what I think you need to note because that is probably the most outstanding difference between the voice of the Lord and the voice of the enemy (evangelistic ministry aside here).

3. The Voice Comes From "Without"

I am just talking purely about the prophetic ministry here. In prophetic ministry, the Lord speaks to you in that soft, gentle voice.

However, the enemy comes to you from without. It seems as though he puts this thought on you from without and it is very strong and forceful so that you feel that you must drop everything and do it right now!

No, the Lord has a very clear time and if He wants you to do something that is important, He will confirm it. Sure there are times when you will feel a prayer burden. You will feel a need and that urgency to go and pray in intercession. Sure, but then you are going to feel it on the inside and after you pray you will feel a lift.

However, when you feel a "push" and you end up coming under guilt, you feel fear and curses start manifesting in your life, be cautious.

4. Curses Start Manifesting

If you responded to that pushy voice, then guess what? The voice that you were listening to was not the voice of the Lord. Unfortunately, when you submit to a deception and when you allow the enemy to speak in your ear and listen to His words, you give him license in your life.

It's like a chain reaction. It is one link in the chain and then another and another an another.

Sure, in between there the Lord gets His voice through to you but the problem is that you have opened the door to the enemy. As long as he has got the key to that door he is in and out of it as often as he wants.

Closing the Door to Deception

What you have to do if you realize that you made that mistake is to submit yourself to the Lord. Do what it says in *James 4:7 Therefore submit to God. Resist the devil and he will flee from you.*

Just say, "Lord, forgive me for obeying the voice of the enemy. I just submit to you now and satan, you loose your hold on me now. I bind you now in the name of Jesus and I am not going to hear your voice anymore. You take your deception and you get out!"

You can even pray that on your own. It is not such a big deal. You can overcome the enemy. You don't have to listen to those words.

In fact, a good guideline to follow is that if at any time you feel that "push" that you have to share the word now, instead of reacting - sit down, shut up and wait.

If you still feel the same way a good while afterwards, then ask the Lord to open the way for you to share, but don't ever feel pushed and shoved!

What if the word is of God and you miss it...?

It does not matter as much as you think it does. You know we had old Elijah sitting there wailing about how tough things were, about how he was the only prophet alive. In the middle of his pity party, the Lord said to him, "I have a couple of thousand others that haven't bowed their knee! You are not the only one."

You Don't Carry the World

Well, the same holds true for you. If you miss it, He is gracious. He has others that He can raise up. He is not dead! The whole world doesn't rest on your shoulders.

I know, as prophets we forget this. We think sometimes that if we don't do it now and if we are not the savior and we don't jump in - the world will stop turning.

Guess what though... God is still God of His Church! It's His Church and it is His Bride... that's why He is God!

We are simply servants doing His bidding and if we don't do His bidding He will raise up another. What is important is that you keep your heart pure before Him. We are all going to miss it! God is God. He can take care of it.

He can even take care of your mistakes if you just had more faith in Him than you did in your weakness and failure!

Yes, you will miss it but so what? Does it really matter? No, it doesn't! What matters is the outcome, and God is in control of that.

So if you have these voices that are pushy, don't run off and give into them. Instead stop and wait for confirmation. Wait until your emotions have died down so you can be sure of the word.

Then when you are sure and God has confirmed and you still feel the anointing, then step out in boldness. Then there is nothing that can stop it. However, if you feel that Thummim, if you feel a mixture, rather wait! The Lord is in control here, not you. If the revelation is of Him, it will come back again gently.

Usually what I find with the voice of the enemy is that it comes very loudly and it comes very strongly. If you resist it though, it usually goes away and then you know that it wasn't the Lord.

The Voice of the Lord

The Scriptures say, *"Behold, I stand at the door and knock. If anyone hears My voice and opens the door, I will come in to him and dine with him, and he with Me." (Revelation 3:20)*

The Lord Jesus is like that. He doesn't come and with a battering ram to bash down your door. He does not stomp into our house, taking your food off the table.

No, He knocks and He waits for you to answer. If you answer, then He comes in. That is His nature and it is really the epitome of what the Lord's voice is like. He won't come as a loud roaring lion.

1. Gentle as Butterflies

Perhaps at the beginning when you are not used to getting revelation yet, you might feel the anointing quite strongly or you might feel like you have butterflies in your stomach.

It might come strongly at the beginning. However, if you find that the manifestations of the anointing are not as strong anymore, relax. It is okay!

It just means that you are growing up. It is normal. At the beginning it is very strong and very intense and it is all very exciting, but it does calm down because you are growing up.

You don't need all the fluff - you don't need all the big stuff to know that this is God speaking to you.

2. The Same Picture Will Repeat

The Lord will speak to you in a gentle voice most of the time. If you are receiving a vision, you will just receive the same vision a few times.

You will feel that stirring in your belly almost like butterflies but not big ones, just little flutters, as you feel an excitement in your spirit.

The picture or words will bring joy and life and you look forward to sharing it. Now that's the voice of the Lord. Of course also, in case you haven't heard this before, it will come with faith, hope and love.

3. Revelation Will Produce Faith, Hope and Love

Without that, how are you going to mature the body of Christ?

So these are some ways that you can use to really discern for yourself what the voice of the Lord is like.

After you have shared, you will see the effects on the people. They should feel closer to the Lord, convicted or having been touched in some way. You will give them hope for the future or the tenacity to hang on no matter what.

4. The Lord Will Confirm

One thing I love about speaking for the Lord is that He is always willing to confirm His word to us. Just look at good old Gideon putting those fleeces before the Lord.

The Lord did not chastise him for it, but proved His will to the man. How much more for you and I in a New Testament Church known as His bride?

You do not need to be afraid to ask the Lord for confirmation when you are speaking on His behalf. He will be only too happy to give it to you through another prophet or even through the person you are ministering to.

Sometimes prophets do have to cut against the grain and share things that people might not want to hear. That does not mean He will leave you stranded though.

The Lord will confirm His word to you. Either you will see the immediate fruit of the word you share or someone else will share something that lines up.

It is especially good if you are able to minister with a team – then each of you can confirm one another. This is certainly how I operate with my own team.

Each one will get a piece of the revelation and so together we will get the full picture.

5. The Doors Open

When the Lord gives you a revelation to share, although it might stretch you at times, you can be sure that it is in your power to deliver. Not only will He anoint you for it, but He will open the doors as well.

When the Lord gives you a revelation, you should not need to bash down any doors. Rather, the Lord will open the doors. All you need to do is make yourself available.

If you have a hunger to be used of the Lord, then all you need to do is make yourself available and to ask the Lord to use you. Leave the door opening to Him.

Not only will He share His heart with you, but the doors will open also. One mistake us over-zealous prophets often make is to think we must bash down every door to deliver the word that God has given to us.

This is not true. The Lord will open the door along with the word. Elijah had the right word just in time for the king to come to the end of himself and be ready for a show down with the prophets of Baal.

It was a perfect word in season and the Lord arranged the circumstances along with the word. If you receive a revelation and the doors are just not opening it could well be that the timing is just not right.

Wait. The word will not suddenly disappear. Rather, it will brew inside of your spirit and by the time you are ready to speak, it will come forth with power!

Consider Mary who held up all the words that she received about Jesus in her heart. She did not go around blabbing to everyone that she was pregnant with the Messiah. She waited on that revelation.

However, after Jesus was resurrected it was time to share those revelations. How else do you think the Gospels were written? Only Mary could have shared how it was for her to get the news and then give birth to Jesus in Bethlehem.

So in the same way, rest assured that the Lord will open the doors for you to speak. You do not need to strive. If the doors do not open, then allow those words to build up in your heart.

When the time is right, you can be sure that they will come forth in power.

6. Flows Like a River

When you share a prophetic word that is clearly the voice of God, it will flow like a river. The Lord might give you a picture or just the first few words of a prophecy and then it is for you to open your mouth and speak.

If the doors are clearly open for you (say for example it is a church meeting and the leader opens the floor to share) then it is for you to step out. When a word is from the Lord, you do not need to stop and think about it.

How to Judge Any Revelation

The pictures and words bubble up from your spirit like rivers of living water. These words do not "stop and start" but they flow into one another.

One picture will end and another will pop up into your spirit. When the visions and words end, then it is time to stop speaking. You will find it hard to prophesy if you are just listening to your head because you will have to think through everything you say.

When the voice is God's you do not have to try and think. In fact, by the time you are done, you will say to yourself, "Wow! That was such an awesome word! That blessed me!"

You will know that the words were not your own, because you had not thought of them before. Not only that, but the words will minister to you as much as everyone else!

Identifying the Three Voices

As you learn to identify this in yourself, you will also learn how to identify it in others.

Somebody will stand up to speak and you will say, "That is coming straight out of his head. There is no spirit or revelation in it!"

You know, that's a very sad state when people who are not spirit filled want to stand up and prophesy. They stand up and talk logic.

You will find this in some denominations that don't believe in speaking in tongues but they believe in prophesying. Well, try to stand up and speak a prophetic word without being baptized with the Holy Spirit - what do you think will come out? Their mind!

Learn to recognize this. Learn to see when somebody is really speaking from the Lord. Is it coming with that gentle flow? Is it coming like rivers of living water?

That is not to say that every prophecy will be nice and gentle, because His sword can also be sharp but the point is it brings with it a hope and expectation. It brings life to you and an expectation as to what God will do!

CHAPTER 04

Common Mistakes of Prophecy Presentation

Chapter 04 – Common Mistakes of Prophecy Presentation

> *2 Peter 1:19 And so we have the prophetic word confirmed, which you do well to heed as a light that shines in a dark place, until the day dawns and the morning star rises in your hearts;*

It was another full day of ministry and clear past midnight before I could finally fall into bed. Tip-toeing to my toddler's bedroom I made my way in the dark to kiss her cheek, pray over her and catch a glimpse of her sleeping face in the moonlight.

All pictures of cute cuddles and kisses flew out the window as I tip-toed ever so carefully, putting my full weight on a piece of Lego left precariously on the floor.

Stumbling around in the dark, I tried to find balance... only to trip over a scooter left in a place no scooter should ever be.

Bumped, bruised and holding my breath so that I did not wake my daughter with my stifled cry, I hobbled out of the room.

Had the light been on, I would have been able to steer clear of the nuclear disaster waiting for me in that bedroom.

This picture, my friends, is no different to what it feels like when you are trying to do the work of the Lord, but have no idea where you are going.

You might have all the good intentions in the world, but if you try to "fly blind" there is no doubt in my mind that you too will find yourself stumbling, fumbling and hobbling from behind that pulpit nursing a bruised ego.

Well, that is where I step in to help. Consider me the one to switch on the light and help you find your way, so that you can express all the love you have for the children of God.

In this teaching I will not be teaching you how to prophesy, because I will assume that you already know all that!

Instead I am going to take what you already have and help you to deliver it in a way that hits the mark every time.

There are some common mistakes that prophets make when it comes to delivering the word that God has given to them.

Trust me today when I say – you do not have to be one of those prophets!

By marking off the pitfalls and sticking close to the clear path I will map out for you, you will easily navigate your way past Lego, scooters and other similar and terrifying obstacles that every prophet faces.

Enlighten Believers

The above Scripture really sums up what a prophetic word and a revelation should do to the heart of the hearer. It should be like a light in a dark dingy room, where before they were walking and they could not see anything.

They were stumbling over things in front of them. They didn't know where they were going. There was confusion, doubt and fear. A prophetic word should be like a light in that room.

When we share what the Lord places in our hearts to share for a specific time and a specific season it should be like walking into that room and just switching on the light, so that the person who hears the word receives understanding.

The doubts leave and the fear goes. They receive faith, hope and love. That is really in essence what a revelation should do to the heart of a hearer.

However, that is not always what happens a lot of the time. Particularly in the body of Christ as the prophetic move has really come in force and prophets are springing up all over the place, it hasn't come about that way.

In this book, I am going to look at some of the wrong and right ways you should be presenting God's revelation. You will also learn how a wrong presentation has brought destruction in the body of Christ, but how a correct presentation has brought life.

I will share what the wrong image looks like and what the right image looks like. And perhaps you can compare yourself. Maybe you can tick them off in your mind and you may think, "Oops, done that; messed up there!"

Effects of Wrong Presentation

I can assure you I have lived a lot of these. I have done all the don'ts. I have done all the "this is what you shouldn't do's" before I got to, "this is the right way." So I know where you are coming from.

As I work through this list and you go, "Oh, I did that. I shouldn't have done that," don't fret about it too much. It is all part of the learning curve. As long as you keep going, keep getting up and moving towards the goal, the Lord will be with you and He will continue to fill your heart.

So let's get right into the nitty-gritty of it and look at what a wrong presentation has done to the Church.

Damnation Prophets Cause Fear

Firstly, we have our hell and damnation prophets. You know the prophets I am speaking of. They say things like, "Turn back to the Lord or He will destroy your church!"

They stand up like John the Baptist with stick in hand, waving and condemning the people of God. What this has done, is brought fear into the body of Christ. A prophet has stood up and said, "If you don't do what God tells you to do, He is going to take your business away from you. If you don't do this and sort out that sin in your life, He is going to destroy you. He's going to take this away. Your child is going to die."

I have heard some scary things that have come out of the mouths of prophets.

"If you don't do what I say and what I tell you God says you must do, this is going to happen to you. That is going to happen to you!"

And so they speak curses on God's people. What it has done is opened the hearts of God's people to fear. Now perhaps you do not know it, but one of the biggest doors to a curse in your life is to open your heart to fear.

And so instead of being a gift to the body of Christ, the prophet has opened the people's hearts to fear, which has indeed brought a curse and all those negative things to take place in the body of Christ. It is totally opposite from the light. They instead brought darkness.

Ours is a God of light and life. He came to reveal the truth and set the captives free! During the birth of the prophetic move prophets were scary to behold! Even to the point where people were afraid of them. They were afraid that all their sin would be exposed in front of everyone. So instead of getting a touch from God, they hid from His hand.

Tactless – We Could Use a Little Salt!

Next, prophets can be tactless. Because we see things in black and white and there is just no in between with us. How often have you found yourself saying, "If that's the way it is, that's just the way it is, and I'm going to say it the way it is and it is for you to accept it."

That might be all fine and well, but sometimes people need to hear things with a little bit of sugar coating. People don't want to hear, "You know what? You're really ugly."

That hurts somebody's feelings. You can stand up and present a word and just say it so tactlessly that it makes people feel uncomfortable. They don't want to listen to you. They want to start backing up into a corner and get out of there. They don't want to see you staring down at them. I am the first in line with this one! I am so confrontational that I often have to remember that there is a better way to say something!

People do not like you to just say things as they are without seasoning those words with a bit of salt.

I love this passage:

> *Colossians 4:6 Let your speech be always with grace, seasoned with salt, that ye may know how ye ought to answer every man. (KJV)*

This is especially true when you are dealing with this issue in exposing people's problems and hurts. When you are training people there are times you have to come to them and say, "You're doing this wrong."

However, there is a way of saying, "You really messed this up and you must stop doing this right now," and a way of saying, "I really feel that the Lord is leading you in a direction where you need to leave this behind and start now moving towards the goal."

That sounds so much nicer than, "You really messed it up. The Lord's telling you to give it up and forget about it."

There is a way of saying things, and maybe this is just people skills. I think there are a lot of prophets out there, and many that I know personally that could really use some good people skills, because they frighten people away.

Nobody wants to receive a word from you. In fact, when you start to talk they are looking for the door and they are out of there.

What you need to share might be good stuff. It may be good food, but they take one look at this and they say, "I just don't want to touch it, because I'm not prepared to face what is going to come out of that guy's mouth."

They are nervous of you. You know the kind of prophets I am talking about. That is not the way God intended it to be. I know He wants us to stand out, but He wants us to stand out to draw people to us, not to make them run for the door.

Rebel With a Cause

Next, prophets have been rebellious. This is also something that all of us have seen. They have been rebellious against authority, and we understand why. We understand that they see things that other people don't see, and they rebel against it.

Unfortunately, though, because of their rebellion and the way that they have done it, it has made people doubt the prophetic ministry in a lot of churches. It has made people look at them and say, "Ooh, I don't know about him. He looks a bit shady. I can't trust him. Did you see the way he treated the pastor publicly, and the way he stands up and just does what he wants to do, and the way he reacts so openly and so overboard?"

The way you have responded makes people look and say, "I don't know, he doesn't look very stable. I don't know if I can open my heart to this person." Now what you may have had to share could have really been of God, but by the way in which you have responded to and reacted against the leadership openly in rebellion, it closes off the hearts of the rest of the church. They don't want to listen to you after that, because they are not sure of you.

They think, "Well if he's in rebellion, he must be in deception. Any word that this guy speaks must be totally out of line. I've seen the way he acts. I've seen the way he reacts against authority. He can't submit to his boss. He can't even submit to his pastor. He can't submit to anybody! I'm not going to open my heart to somebody like that."

And so they close their hearts off to what could have really been a powerful word from God. But you see, once again the presentation, the seed truth was there. The seed of what you had to share was there, but the way in which it was presented was wrong.

Fortune-Telling

This next failure has been devastating to the body of Christ, is the fact that a prophet has become like a fortune-teller. A prophet no longer brings the light into a dark room. A prophet comes in and says, "You have another room, and it is filled with every good thing of gold and silver and gemstones - and that new Mercedes you've been wanting." And so the prophet has become a fortune-teller.

"The Lord tells me you must marry Peter, and that he is going to give you a house in the hills."

"The Lord tells me that you are going to have a million dollars."

"The Lord tells me that you must become a lawyer."

The prophet has become a fortune-teller, and it was never ever what God intended. God never intended for the prophet to stand up and tell people their future. It didn't work that way in the Old Testament, and it still doesn't work that way today.

Samuel didn't go up to David and say, "David, the Lord tells me you're going to get that silver-lined chariot that you have been desiring." Did you ever see that in the Scriptures? I didn't see it there. The Lord spoke blessing and He spoke confirmation, but He was never a fortune-teller to tell people their futures.

"You're going to have three kids – two girls and a boy."

Unfortunately, that is what it has come to in the body of Christ today, and it has destroyed the true work of the prophet, because people have been hurt. People have been disappointed. I cannot tell you how many times I have had people write to me and say, "This prophet prophesied that the Lord has given me a new house, and it never came to pass."

"A prophet prophesied to me that the Lord was going to give me a new car and that I was going to write a book, that I was going to be famous, and it never happened, so God must have lied. God doesn't want to give it to me, therefore I turn my back on God."

Prophets Don't Have a Magic Wand

How many times have you seen that? I have seen many times, how people are holding onto a prophetic word. They write it out and they repeat it every day. They say, "Oh, please can it come to pass. Please Lord," and it never happens. Why?

It is because God never intended for a prophet to be a fortune-teller. God intended for a prophet to give confirmation and to stir up the hearts of God's people, not to turn their eyes away from Him.

It has destroyed and has broken down faith, hope and love. It has taken the incentive away from the individual believer to believe on their own behalf. People want a magic wand so they go to the prophets.

We see it all the time as we minister to prophets in our ministry. People say, "I want you to pray for me that my finances will just come right." Or, "I'm having serious problems with my spouse right now. They're in rebellion. My wife is off doing her own thing. I want you to pray that she sorts herself out."

"My children are running off and disobeying me. I want you to pray that they just come right."

They want you to just stand there and wave a magic wand.

You say, "Yes, but do you know that you are the result of why your children are running off?"

"There is perhaps something wrong with you, that your wife doesn't want anything to do with you?"

They don't want to hear that. They want a magic wand. And unfortunately the prophets who have been fortune-telling have encouraged this. They have encouraged the people to be reliant on them for every step of their future.

There are some people who cannot take a single step without going to the prophet to find out if this is of God. They have become so dependent on the prophetic word that they can't make a single move in their lives without it.

"I don't want to be out of God's will. Tell me, is this right? Is this wrong? Must I marry so-and-so or mustn't I marry him? Must I have another child, or not?"

I am not saying that we shouldn't go to God for those things. What I am saying is that the body of Christ should not be dependent on the prophet for those things.

They should be dependent on God for those things to hear for themselves. Because the prophet has been seen as the seer, the fortune-teller, people come to the fortune-teller to have their fortunes read to them.

It has become no different to the New Age movement, to psychics and tarot card readers. If there is one thing I stand against very firmly, it is that, because I see this element in nearly every prophet that comes to us and is untrained.

They think that the prophet is only there to give words of wisdom, to tell the people about their future. Unless that future involves Jesus Christ, there is no future for them at all. No, the call of the prophet is to teach people to hear God for themselves. It burns in me to introduce the Bride to her Savior.

That way, believers can ask God for themselves! We do so much teaching on how to hear the Lord for yourself, that I will not belabor the point here. The bottom line? You are not the only source to God as a prophet. Rather, you are the mediator to bring the Bride to Jesus and to rejoice when they are united!

Right Word, Wrong Time

Prophets bring words in the wrong timing. We have seen this. You stand up and the Lord gives you a word for the leadership of a church. So while you are all upset and full of anger you stand up and share that word.

Right word, Wrong time! A word has a time and a season, and you should be very sensitive as to when to share a word. You see, a person's heart has to be ready to receive, and if you stand up to share at the wrong time their heart is not ready and the word is like the seed of the sower, which is thrown away onto the stone, or where the birds can pick it up, or by the thorns. It just dies. It never sprouts or takes root.

You have to speak a word at the right time, and so many words have been spoken at the wrong times. I have learned this one the hard way. The Lord gives me a powerful revelation and I think, "Everybody's got to hear this! Everybody that hears this word is just going to say, 'Wow, you're such an incredible prophet! That is the best word I ever heard. This is going to go international.'"

I can't wait to get out there and let everybody know, and not even a single person responds to it. Why? It was shared at the wrong time. They weren't ready to receive it yet.

But yet I have noticed that a couple of months down the line suddenly other prophets start getting the same word as me, and everybody raves about it. I think, "Hmm, they didn't say a thing when I brought that word. Nobody even noticed. What's so special about them? They didn't even present it as well as I did."

That is because it was shared in the wrong time. You have to share the right word at the right time, because the hearts of God's people are like a garden, and that garden has to be ready for those seeds to be planted into it. If in that garden the soil is hard and it hasn't been watered or plowed yet, you can't go trying to shove your seed into it. It is not going to happen.

That is why the prophet should always be submitting to the Spirit, always know, see and feel where to go and where not to go.

Be Sensitive to the Spirit

We should be sensitive to the Holy Spirit twenty-four hours a day, not just when we are standing up to give a prophetic word. We should always know when to speak and when to shut up.

Most times it is when to shut up, because I think prophets speak too much at times. I know about it. I am the expressive. I am forever putting my foot in it. I have my foot more often in my mouth than I do on the floor, and I have had to learn that when I feel a knot in my stomach the Lord is saying, "Shut up!"

"But Lord, it's such a good word."

"Shut up!"

"They're going to love it, Lord. Can't I just give them two words?"

"Keep quiet! Now is not the time."

The time will come, and when I share it in the right timing it always bears fruit.

Revelation on Demand

Now we have revelation on demand, which is something similar to fortune-telling. Anybody who has studied our prophetic school will know my personal feelings on giving a prophetic word on demand. How many times (yet again) have we seen people writing, "I need you to give me a prophetic word. I need to move jobs and I need you to give me a prophetic word."

"I would like to start up a new ministry, and I need you to give a prophetic word."

So now we must sit down and do the prophetic thing, let the anointing come down and get a prophetic word? No, we're not psychics. We're prophets, and there is a big difference between being a psychic and being a prophet.

We are prophets and we move when the Holy Spirit moves us. The Word says that the Holy Spirit manifests the gifts to whom He wills to manifest them, and those gifts are used for the body of Christ. And if He decides He would like to speak to somebody through us, then He moves us.

> *1 Corinthians 12:10 To another the working of miracles; to another prophecy; to another discerning of spirits; to another divers kinds of tongues; to another the interpretation of tongues:*
> *11 But all these worketh that one and the selfsame Spirit, dividing to every man severally **as he will**.*
> *(KJV)*

We do not move ourselves. We can make ourselves available. We can say, "Lord, is there anything you want to say to this person?" The minute you start looking for revelation on demand though, you are looking for deception, because if you want a revelation, you are surely going to get it.

You will get it, but I can't guarantee that you will be getting it from the Lord. I can't guarantee that it will be inspired by the Word.

Charging for Words

Perhaps this is so common that no one even looks sideways at it any longer. However, I will never forget the first time I came across this phenomenon in the Church.

I was so shocked to browse the Internet and there was a ministry offering saying, "Your own directive personal prophetic word for $25.00!"

"You'll get your own 15-minute cassette mailed to your door for $25.99 – your prophetic word. We will wait on God on your behalf and get a word just for you!"

Do you know what is even more shocking? People are buying it! They are paying for it, because everybody wants a fortune-teller. Nobody has learned to hear the voice of God for themselves, and that is where the prophetic ministry has erred. I will get to that later on.

Prophesying Your Own Burdens

The prophetic ministry has brought a great confusion to the body of Christ, because they have prophesied their own burdens. We get some people coming in who are a total mess. They say, "This person prophesied that I'm an evangelist. This person prophesied that I'm a prophet. This person prophesied that I'm a pastor. This person prophesied that I'm a teacher. What am I? I don't know whether I'm coming or going, up or down or what is going on."

They are running around collecting all these prophetic words and none of them agree! They are in total confusion and they are standing bewildered going, "What now? Where do I go? I can't even see the road in front of me."

The prophet has prophesied his own burden. You have the evangelist with a burden for evangelism saying, "The Lord is calling you to go and win the lost."

You have the prophet, who has a burden for psalmody and he is saying, "You're called to be a psalmist."

You have the teacher, who has a burden for the Word, and he is saying, "I believe the Lord is telling you, you must get more into the Word."

That wasn't revelation. That was your own burden! Be careful that you do not look at somebody and assess them and say, "I know just what they need to hear. I've got just the thing for them."

The reality is that God's people don't need to hear what the prophet has for them. They need to hear what God has for them.

Bringing Balance

We had one couple who thought they were doing us a favor by sending us all the prophetic words they had ever been given. There were pages and pages of them. I don't know why they thought we wanted to read all this, but you should have seen the mess. We are not even talking little nobody prophets here. We are talking about some big name ministries.

In one word the Lord had called them to raise money for the church. Somebody else said, "No, the Lord has called you to be evangelists." Somebody else said that the Lord had called them to be missionaries. Yet another person said, "The Lord has called you to a children's ministry. I really feel you need to minister there."

It was a mess, and these people thought, "Well, we must be so good that the Lord has called us to do everything!"

We had to break it to them and say, "Burn the prophetic words! Stop basing your life on prophetic words and base your life on the Word of God, because that is unchanging."

Not Word-Based

I don't know how many times I've heard people prophesy, "The Lord has called you to raise money for the church."

What kind of spiritual gift does it take to raise money? What kind of gift is that, but yet you are called to the ministry of money-making? I have heard this prophesied so many times over people. Why? It is because they want some money, so they think, "If I prophesy over you that you're going to make money for the church, you're going to start sowing into my ministry."

You see, they are prophesying their burden and what they had in mind. It has destroyed the body of Christ. It has broken down the foundation of the Word that is in them. It has left them fleeting and running here and there on things that have no solid foundation.

Then when they leave that place and they try and live their lives, those words are like sand. They are like the man who built his house on the sand, and they wash away. The first rainstorm that comes and that house is laid flat, because the prophet did not prophesy the Word of God. He prophesied his own burden.

Paul says in 1 Corinthians 14:39-40

> *Therefore, brethren, desire earnestly to prophesy, and do not forbid to speak with tongues.*
> *40 Let all things be done decently and in order.*

If every prophet were truly hearing from God, all things would be done decently and in order, because our God is a God of order, not of confusion. If any word is bringing confusion, then that word is not of God.

CHAPTER 05

Getting Prophecy Presentation Right!

Chapter 05 – Getting Prophecy Presentation Right!

Effects of Correct Presentation

Now that I have depressed you and absolutely destroyed the prophetic ministry so that nobody wants to touch that smelly prophet anymore, we are going to look at what the correct presentation has done to the Church and restore some of the hope.

The truth is that the Lord has given the prophet as a gift to the Church. We are meant to bring the fragrance of Christ – a sweet smelling savor into the Church. So let's see what we can do to make that a reality in your ministry shall, we?

It says in Ephesians 1:17:

> *That the God of our Lord Jesus Christ, the Father of glory, may give to you the spirit of wisdom and revelation in the knowledge of Him,*

Revelation of Jesus

Notice the words, "in the knowledge of Him". The body of Christ has come to know the Lord Jesus through the prophetic ministry, because the prophet has a burning desire to enter into an intimate relationship with the Lord Jesus.

The prophet is never satisfied to just know "of the Lord". The prophet wants to know the Lord personally, and his desire and passion to know the Lord has opened the eyes of the body of Christ to a relationship with Jesus. Because of the prophetic ministry, Christianity is no longer just a religion.

You see, the prophet says, "This is reality. This isn't religion. This isn't just do's and don'ts. This isn't just rules. It is the real stuff."

The prophets have come to know the move of the Spirit and hear the Lord's voice. They see Him as somebody real and so they shared that with the body of Christ. We are now starting to see a new awareness of the Lord all over the world. A new relationship between the groom and the bride is starting to develop.

Before this move, people went to church every Sunday and it was a staid, religious experience. It has been like this for centuries. You will especially notices this, if you look at the history of the Church right through Catholicism and all of the different changes.

However, as the prophetic move came into the body of Christ an explosion of entering into a deeper relationship with Christ and an awareness of, "This isn't something that I do. This is something that I have. This isn't a set of rules. This is a real relationship," started.

Opened Church's Eyes

And so the body of Christ's eyes have been opened to Jesus, and the bride is being prepared for the end times. The spots and the wrinkles are starting to be taken away, because the bride is starting to fall in love with her groom. It is when the bride falls in love with her groom that she gets ready for Him.

The prophetic movement has taken the body of Christ a great leap forward in preparing it to meet the groom. True revelation has opened up their eyes in their spiritual lives. Not too long ago, people didn't even believe in speaking in tongues. If you did, you were considered demonized - it was that bad. With the prophetic movement coming into the Church though, people's eyes have been opened to the spiritual realm.

People have begun to realize, "Hey, there is more to living this Christian life than rules. We have authority in the name of Jesus Christ. We can come to Him and receive from Him. We can hear His voice for ourselves."

They are being exposed to it and are saying, "He can speak to me in dreams and visions. I can receive from Him. I can know when to make a decision in my life and when not to, just by hearing His voice.

There is something deeper to this thing than just a nametag. When I call myself a Christian it is not just a nametag, it is who I am. There's a whole spiritual realm that is at my disposal. The angels are helping me.

They're setting the path straight before me as the Word says. There's more to this whole thing."

Explosion of Word and Spirit

It has opened up the eyes of the body of Christ to a deeper realm. As a result, the Word that has been in the hearts of every believer all along is now being ignited by the Spirit.

The Word has been preached through the generations and has remained solid as a rock. However, now suddenly the Spirit has come upon that Word and an explosion is taking place in the hearts of God's people.

Before people just knew it in their heads. It was just Scriptures and it was a case of, "Oh, I know the Scriptures." They could even quote a few scriptures, but it was all in their heads. As the prophet started opening their eyes to the spiritual realm though, it started sinking into their hearts.

People are saying, "I'm not settling for second best anymore. I'm sick of being run down. I'm sick of the enemy ruling my life. I'm sick of poverty. I'm sick of this mess. I'm sick of broken marriages and my family being in trouble all the time."

Now they are taking the water in their hearts and the knowledge in their heads and are igniting it. Suddenly the enemy is running, because now he is coming against believers, who don't say, "Oh well, it's God's will that we suffer."

Instead they are saying, "Oh no! In the name of Jesus, I bind you satan, because this is my right." They are learning to use their spiritual authority that has been there all along.

The prophetic ministry has helped to make people realize that Jesus is on their side. They have more than head knowledge now. They have power in their spirits. And so a tremendous awakening has started in the body of Christ.

Psalmody, Praise and Worship

There has been an explosion in psalmody and praise and worship. You just need to look at the body of Christ ten years ago and now to see the change that has taken place in praise and worship.

A few years back, everybody had their little hymnals. They would put the songs on the overhead, sing them and smile and say, "Oh we had such a lovely time at church today. We sang a few songs. Then we listened to the preacher, and then we went home."

It is not like that anymore. We have seen an explosion in praise and worship. Churches are having concerts. The youth is going nuts. They are dancing, praising and singing. There is prophetic dance and prophetic music. "Prophetic everything" has come into the Church and people are starting to enter into a realm of music that they had never entered into before.

Something incredible has been birthed in Christian music, and I firmly believe that a great move is coming in the way of music and dance. Actually, it has already begun. Suddenly the Lord is touching people and they are breaking out in spontaneous praise and worship.

Continuous Praise

The prophetic ministry has brought that about, because it is the prophet who knows how to bring the presence of God through music. It is their desire and passion for music that has brought this to the body of Christ.

Now we have twenty-four hour sessions of praise and worship going on in centers all over the world. It is not strange to hear of that kind of thing happening anymore.

I remember talking about a vision we had before the prophetic ministry was even a phrase used in the Church. We said, "Could you imagine a place where there is twenty-four hour praise and worship, all the time?" It was such a big, "Wow, imagine!" For years it was a case of, "Wow! Imagine! What if...?"

Now it's here. It's happening. People's hearts are being stirred towards praising, dancing, singing and clapping. Everything that has breath is praising the Lord. The prophetic ministry brought that about. It brought that life into the body of Christ that had been lacking for so many years.

Words of Wisdom

Also, the words of wisdom spoken by the prophets have given people hope. This isn't fortune-telling. It is a case of, "The Lord is with you, and if you go through that door He is going to bless what you put your hand to.

Don't worry, the Lord has the situation in control. You're going to do well. Do what's in your heart to do. The Lord will be with you."

It has given people hope because they wanted to go in a direction but they were not sure. They needed to know, "Should I take this step or shouldn't I?" So the prophet came along and said, "The Lord says that He is going to be with you and that it is of Him. Go for it." It has given them hope. It has given them something to aim towards and given them direction.

Inner Healing

Also, the words of knowledge have brought healing to the body of Christ. Another great movement that has emerged is that of inner healing. The prophetic ministry has introduced inner healing to the body of Christ. Why is this? It is because the prophet gets revelation.

He says, "I see you at the age of five. Something happened round about that time in your life."

The person says, "Yes, this and that happened."

The prophet then speaks healing into that memory. As a result of this ministry, Christians no longer have to walk around with all these hurts in their lives.

The prophets spoke life and brought change. People started to realize, "I don't have to carry this baggage around with me anymore. I can truly come to the cross and let it go. I can do this."

The prophetic ministry has brought the ministry of inner healing to the Church. This was probably one of the very first signs to the body of Christ that the prophetic ministry was bringing change. Inner healing came first and it was followed by spiritual revelation, praise and worship, and the intimate relationship with Jesus.

The prophetic ministry helped remove all the blockages that were preventing God's people from flowing out of their spirit.

Their hurts prevented them from expressing the Spirit of God. All the pain and hurt, rejection and abuse – that baggage that they carried around – the prophet spoke life and took that baggage away. Once they were free they were then open to not only receive from God but to also give to God.

And so we have people walking around today who are free, who have given up that bondage and who are released, because of what the prophetic ministry has accomplished in their lives.

This is God's true purpose for the prophet – to bring healing, life, change and an explosion into the body of Christ. It is not to bring death, but to bring life.

True Faith

The revelation the prophet brought has inspired faith, hope and love in the body of Christ. People have come to love the Lord. They now see a future goal. All that knowledge of the Word of God that has been in their heads all along has been converted to true faith, not just head knowledge.

The word that the prophet spoke produced faith in the hearts of God's people.

Many people have been believing and crying out to the Lord for things. "Lord, I really need this in my life."

Maybe, they were believing Him for a child or another need or desire.

It's the function of the prophet to say to someone like that, "The Lord tells me that whatever it is that you have been believing Him for, He is going to provide it for you." That confirmation is the faith this person needed, to release it so it could come to pass.

Fortune-Telling vs. Word of Wisdom

You see, there is a difference between fortune-telling and confirmation. Fortune-telling says, "The Lord says you're going to have a car," and you go, "Wow, I never thought of that before! That would be really nice. I could use a nice new car." That is fortune-telling.

Confirmation through a word of wisdom says, "The Lord tells me you have been believing for a car."

They respond, "How did you know? I have really been desiring this of the Lord. I have been seeking His face about this. We have needed it badly."

That is confirmation. If I don't hear a confirmation when I tell somebody something, I know I missed it. If I say to somebody, "I believe the Lord is telling you this," and they say, "I never thought about that before…" I think, "I missed it!"

The word that comes out of a prophet's mouth should not be something that you haven't heard before. It should be something that has always been in your heart, but the word caused it to come to life in you. That is what a prophetic word should do.

CHAPTER 06

The Image of Prophetic Ministry

Chapter 06 – The Image of Prophetic Ministry

The image of the prophet has changed a lot over the years. I would have to say that we all started out a bit zealously when the prophetic move first really started having an impact on the Church.

In many ways we were like kids in a candy store! So full of excitement at the variety and completely wound up on a sugar buzz, good intentions often left a mess behind.

Perhaps you will recognize some aspects that have given the prophetic ministry a bitter taste in the mouth of the Church. From there though, we will tackle the problem together and see how we can bring back the sweet savor of Christ again!

Wrong Presbyteries

Let's have a look now at the incorrect image of the New Testament prophet. You could probably name a couple of these and your mind might go back to some images that you have seen of what a prophet should not look like.

Firstly, you have wrong prophetic presbyteries. You have somebody standing there and they go around like an auctioneer.

"The Lord says you will work with your hands."

When he stops the next person says, "The Lord says you're going to write. You're going to be a writer and you're going to be famous."

Another person says, "The Lord says you're being raised to bring in money for ministries."

Yet another one says, "The Lord has called you to be an evangelist, and you're still called to raise money! The Lord's called you to be a business apostle."

They just ramble on and on and on and fill the person's head with words. When they leave they have to take a recording of the words, because for the life of them they can't remember a single phrase of it!

They go home, write it down and read it and go, "Wow, that's pretty good stuff."

However, there is no change in their hearts. They are not any closer to God. They are not any closer to their goal because of it. All they received was a head full of words. None of it was real.

It was that sand on which the house was built. A prophetic word is not there to tickle the ears. It is not there to fill their head with words. It is there to bring change. It must be that light in the dark room. Unless you are going in and switching on a light, don't waste your time.

People don't want to hear a pile of words. It has done the body of Christ a disservice, because it has destroyed what the true prophetic ministry is there for.

It has destroyed the element of truth and change that should be there. It has made people come to God to receive a pile of words, and then when the words don't come to pass they say, "God is not a man of His word. He doesn't pay up."

I tell you why He didn't pay up. It was because it wasn't His word in the first place. They mumbled a load of garbage that came from their minds. They took a look at the person, assessed them and thought, "They look like they're this sort of person," and then they told them what they wanted to hear.

Worldly Assessment

There was one case I heard which really blew me away. A woman wrote and said, "I went to a prophetic presbytery. I sat down and they started ministering to me, and one of the prophets asked me, 'So what job do you do?' "

She said, "I am a hairdresser."

He said, "I feel that your ministry is going to line up with hairdressing," and he started applying a whole lot of spiritual verbiage to her job, because he didn't have anything to go on. He didn't get a prophetic word so he thought, "Well, I've got to use something."

"What job do you do? You know the Lord often calls us to do things that are related to our jobs."

With her being a hairdresser he probably thought, "Oh Lord, couldn't she have been something else? That's a tough one to use."

You should have heard the nonsense he spoke. He tried to say, "As you're sitting with people and you're doing their hair, this is how you will be applying the Spirit."

I looked at this and I thought, "Oh Lord, what a load of nonsense!" It was because he tried to get revelation on demand.

"Let's tell this person something really good so that on the way out they will put a good check in the box. They're paying for this service, you know."

You think it is a joke that some people charge $25 dollars for a prophetic word? How many people go to these great big conferences and a prophet says, "$200 for a word," and they get up and pay it! Don't laugh. It happens. They don't say it quite that bluntly or that obviously, but that is exactly what it means.

False Payment

There was one lady that we had been ministering to for a long period of time and we had really been pouring into her. She had sown into us, but she really was destitute. She hardly had anything, and all she could give us was $5.00.

You know, it was the biggest amount in our eyes, because it was the only $5.00 that she had, and she sowed it. The Lord immediately gave her a hundredfold return!

She started increasing and increasing until she was giving more like $50.00, and the Lord kept sowing back. We sent her a pile of materials and it was just so wonderful to see the Lord work. Then we didn't hear from her in a while, and she came back and needed us to pray for her.

She said, "I went to this big conference and there was a prophet there who was asking for $200 and he would give a prophetic word. The Lord assured me that I wasn't giving to a man, I was giving to an anointing."

And so she gave all the money that she had to this prophet, and she said, "I don't understand, but ever since he prophesied over me everything has gone wrong in my life. I lost my house. The car broke down. The kids are going crazy. I don't know what is happening.

I need you guys to pray for me, because he prophesied that the Lord was giving me a new car, and he prophesied to me that the Lord was giving me more money. But yet ever since he's prophesied to me everything has gone wrong!"

We had to break the news to her, "Firstly my sister, you could have come and we would have spoken over you for free. Secondly, this prophet has spoken a curse. He has obviously got a curse in his life and when he spoke over your life you got his curse. So you paid $200.00 for a curse!"

People are doing it and they are paying. Can you see how the prophetic ministry has destroyed what it is really meant to do? It has cut down and broken apart. We need to bring change. We need to show people the truth, and we need to stand up and say, "This is it!" We need to be bold about it, because the false prophets are being bold about it and they are leading God's people astray.

So many prophets are sitting in a corner and saying, "Oh Lord, I won't say anything. They won't listen to me anyway."

Well, while you are sitting with that attitude the false prophets are standing up there all bold and leading God's people astray.

They have the boldness to stand up and say what they want to say. But we are too afraid and too shy to stir or to make waves. It is time the true prophets of God rise up and say what needs to be said, telling the truth and bringing the real change.

Instead of cowering and backing off all the time we need to stand up in the power of the Spirit and under the anointing, and speak the truth and bring the change that needs to come. As God's true prophet, they will bring change in the body of Christ and they will steer everyone onto the correct path again.

Kept Babies

Due to the dependency the body of Christ has formed with the prophet, God's children have remained as babies. You know the prophet is saying, "I'm so sick of church. This pastor is forever feeding milk. These people are staying babies all their lives. I'm leaving here because they are just not mature enough for me."

But yet that same prophet will have, people dependent on them for prophetic words. You are doing the same thing. You are keeping God's people babies, because you are keeping them dependent on you instead of dependent on God. You have people running to the prophet every five minutes for words.

We have the same person over and over asking, "Please interpret this dream." They are continually asking, "Please can I receive? Please can I receive? Please pray for me."

If they are in our School I say, "No, we will not pray for you. You learn to pray for yourself!"

It is not because I don't want to give them my ministry, but it is because they must learn to walk. When your child is learning to walk you move away the furniture so they can stand on their own, because while they are still holding on they will never learn to walk for themselves.

The same prophet who has condemned the pastor for always preaching milk is the same prophet who keeps the children of God babies, because they keep them dependent on them.

It feeds the need for acceptance and recognition. It is nice having all these people looking up to me and thinking I'm so wonderful. It is nice having them run to me, and I just give a word and they go, "Wow, you're so incredible. I wish I could hear from God like you."

We have babies. What is the fivefold ministry given to the body of Christ for? For the maturing – the bringing up and growing up – of the saints of God.

> *Ephesians 4:12 For the perfecting of the saints, for the work of the ministry, for the edifying of the body of Christ: (KJV)*

But yet the prophets have made the same mistake as the pastors. They have kept the body of Christ babies, and so there has been no growth. The prophets that have done it right on the other hand have imparted and given strength, have brought growth and have brought maturity.

Persecution Complex

Now let's deal with this bad image of the prophet - the guy who has the persecution complex.

If you have been around prophets you will have heard the guy that says, "I've been kicked out of every church I went to. Every time I try and share with somebody they reject me. I go to work and the people there are picking on me. I can't make friends, because nobody understands me. I must be so spiritual and on such a different plain that I must be the only one that is right in this world."

What you have my friend... is a persecution complex. When somebody comes to me like that I say, "It didn't enter your mind just for a split second that not just everybody in this world is wrong and you're the only one that's right? It didn't enter your mind that maybe you have something to do with this rejection? You don't think so?"

People don't just reject you for the sake of rejecting. They are rejecting you because there is something to reject, and it comes back to how you present yourself.

If somebody comes to me and says, "I get rejected everywhere I go. I must be a prophet," you don't know the death that is awaiting you. You are not the only one who is right and everybody else is wrong. I hate to break it to you, but you have some flesh in there that needs to be crucified.

The prophet with the persecution complex is the wrong image, but we have seen a lot of those. And again, it has given a wrong impression in the mind of God's people of what a prophet really is.

There is however, a good image and a correct image. Paul says in 1 Timothy 4:14

Do not neglect the gift that is in you, which was given to you by prophecy with the laying on of the hands of the eldership.

Correct Presbytery

We see the presbytery here again, but we see something different. It says, "...which was given to you through prophecy, with the laying on of hands." What was given to him? The spiritual gifts were given to him when the presbytery came to town.

He didn't receive a load of words and knowledge, but he received spiritual gifts. Something was planted in his heart that he took away with him.

This is the correct presbytery, when somebody comes and receives something real. When they go away and the storms come, the seed that has been planted within them stands sure.

The word comes back to them and they say, "Oh no, I'm not going to take this storm. I'm going to stand against it with the Word of God." That is because of what has been put inside of them. They go away changed.

They go away with a new impartation, a new gift and a new direction. They don't have to go home and write down the prophetic word. It doesn't matter, because that word wasn't spoken into their head. It was spoken into their heart. The Holy Spirit came in and caused change to take place.

It doesn't matter whether they remember it or not. It really doesn't matter, because the change was done in their heart. They came, received healing or maybe even the baptism of the Holy Spirit. They received gifts and impartations.

They received ministries. They go away with those things inside of their hearts, not inside of their heads. They don't need to remember what the prophet said. Honestly, nine times out of ten they don't remember what was said anyways. But what they will keep with them is the change that took place within.

Changed People

How many presbyteries have you seen that do that, where the person gets up and their face looks different? There is something new there. There is a shine that wasn't there before. There is a hope that wasn't there before. Change has taken place. When you meet that person again a couple of months later they look and act differently.

You say, "Man, I see such a change in you."

I cannot tell you how many prophets have come to us for training that have gone to Conference after Conference, presbytery after presbytery, to receive all these words, which they keep in thick files.

They have all these words and they are still in the same spot they were in thirty years ago. They are not prophesying. They are not standing up and using their authority. They haven't got boldness. Nothing has come of it and nothing has changed. So tell me, what did those words do? They just took up space in that folder. That's all they did. There never produced change.

I expect to see change in the people I minister to, because I am not coming here to fill your head with rubbish. When I speak, that word is not going into your head. It is going into your heart, and whether you understand it or not is also irrelevant, because I am speaking under the power of the Holy Spirit and you are going to change!

When I see you again I expect to see change, not because of me, but because I know that the word went into your heart. I know that the Holy Spirit spoke life into you. That is what we should be seeing with presbyteries. We should see people walking away changed, and we should see them a few months later and not recognize who they are.

We should say, "My goodness you've changed! Wow."

Some people have been with us to see a lot of these transformations, and it is so exciting to meet with somebody again and to see the change in them. I look at our first conference that we ever had in 1999.

We caught everybody on video and they got to stand up and speak. Now at the second one, the people who came again stood up to speak once again. We couldn't believe that they were the same people. There was just something about them that had changed. There was a new boldness, and a new authority.

Do you know what that did to us? We thought, "Wow, we did something. We actually accomplished change in the life of another." There was fruit from that time. That is what makes it worth it. That fruit is what keeps us going.

Releases Into People

A prophet speaks words of life and releases ministries. People have desires in their hearts. They come to us and we say, "That desire that you have had for being a pastor is of God," and we release it into them. People should be released into their ministries.

It is not enough to just say, "The Lord has called you to be an evangelist. The Lord has called you to be something else." They don't want to hear what the Lord has called them to do. They want to be released to do what God has called them to do.

They have the gifts. The Holy Spirit will empower them. From the day they were born again they had the potential in them. You don't need to tell them what's in there. You need to tell them how to use it.

They already have all the gems. They already have everything they need. They have already heard a hundred times about what God has called them to do. They want to know, "How do I do it? How do I get released? How do I start? How do I get going?"

You can't float around your whole life being told you are going to be a pastor or that you are going to be a prophet. You need somebody to come in and say, "Do it. This is how you do it," and so you speak into their lives and release them into that ministry.

You allow the Holy Spirit to come upon them and enable them to do that ministry. Everybody has that potential within them. It is up to the prophet to release that potential in them. That is what the true prophetic ministry should be doing.

Then once again there is inner healing. The prophetic ministry should be bringing healing, bringing change and helping people let go of their baggage. Can you see what a true prophet should look like? He is one that is giving direction; one that is giving insight; one that is speaking into the heart of man to bring change, so that when that person leaves they leave changed. Can you see the two images of how wrong it has been and how right it should be?

CHAPTER 07

Do's & Don'ts of Prophetic Presentation

Chapter 07 – Dos & Don'ts of Prophetic Presentation

I want to go over a list now on the do's and don'ts of presenting a prophetic word. I want you to think of yourself. I want you to think of any time you have had the opportunity to share with anybody.

You don't need to be a prophet to be able to share a revelation. The Lord speaks to us all, whether it be revelation by the word as a teacher, or whether it be revelation through vision, prophecy or any of the gifts. So don't limit yourself and think, "I'm not a prophet. It's not for me."

This is for everybody on how you present what God has given you. God has given us all something – whether you are an evangelist, pastor, teacher, prophet or apostle, He has given you something to share.

Don'ts of Presenting Prophecy

Let's start with the don'ts.

No Mumbling

Don't speak fast and mumble. We have covered this in the preaching and teaching course. Nobody can understand a word you are saying if you are speaking so fast and you're mumbling. This is especially relevant to people from other countries who do not know what you are saying.

With my South African accent, I had to learn this one. People kept on saying to me, "Huh?" I think the best way that the Lord got me to learn this was when He sent Craig and I to Switzerland.

For the entire time we were there we had to work through a translator. Have you ever tried to prophesy through a translator? I certainly learned proper elocution!

Nothing kills the fire of a passionate prophecy more than someone stopping you in the middle of it to say, "Sorry what did you say? I do not know what that word means."

And so we had to learn to speak clearly, softly and use simple words that everyone could understand. Although I kicked against this a lot at the beginning, I look back now and see how integral it was to my training.

Speak slowly, clearly and loudly so that everybody in the room can hear - especially when you are speaking to people who are not of the same nationality as you.

You want them to hear what you said. If they don't hear you they are not going to get it. If they don't get it, they are not going to take it home with them. So make sure they can hear what you are saying.

Don't Apologize for Your Presence

Never apologize for your presence. Never stand and say, "Well, I really hope you'll hear me today. Please, this is a good word. You're going to love this word. Please listen to me."

People will be out the door when you do that. They don't want to listen to you! Nobody wants to follow a sheep. They want to follow a shepherd. So stand up and look like a shepherd.

Don't look like a sheep. Stand up and look like you know what you are doing, even if you don't. Even if you don't have a clue and you are thinking, "Lord, you've given me two words? I've got to stand up with two words?" They don't know that, so stand up and look as though you have it all in hand.

Also, command presence. Make them look at you, because then their hearts will be open to receive. You see, they respect somebody like that. They respect somebody with boldness. That is why the Lord called the church sheep. They want a shepherd. They need one. And if you want them to be changed make sure they are looking at you. Be bold and confident.

Dress for the King

Do not get up looking sloppy. Contrary to popular belief, first impressions do count. So be neat and tidy. Present a good image, because you are standing up to represent Christ!

People will have a hard time respecting somebody that is scruffy and shows signs of not having showered in a week. I know that when I see somebody like that standing up, and I even have the gift of discerning of spirits, I still think, "Not good." It's human nature.

When somebody is looking scruffy you do not want to be around them. You feel uncomfortable next to them. Be presentable. I am not saying you should go overboard, but be presentable.

Don't think, "Oh well, this is just the way I am. They must accept me."

No, they won't. They will lose out on what God has given you to share, just because of that one thing. It may seem small, but it is also important.

Dump Your Hobbyhorse

Next, never speak logical revelation. Don't look at somebody, sum them up and say, "They look like they could be a good teacher." Don't speak from your mind. Speak from the Spirit. Don't carry on in your own hobbyhorse.

Don't feel bad if this is you, because I am also very guilty of this. The Lord gives me a revelation, and this is my hobbyhorse for the month. And every time somebody comes to me I say, "You know what you need to hear...?" and off I go on with my hobby horse.

How often have we done that? Don't do it though, because this person might not really care two hoots about your hobbyhorse and they might not need to hear it right now.

You know many a prophet has the "music hobby horse."

"Everybody should be a musician."

"Everybody should be able to praise and worship."

But you know, some people like to whistle. We know someone who does that. Now, my little hobbyhorse is music and singing so I say, "What's wrong with you man? Why can't you play a musical instrument and sing or something?"

He says, "Well, I just like to whistle."

But you know, singing is my hobbyhorse so I am going to impose my will on him and say, "Don't whistle – sing!"

You know what? It doesn't work for him. Each one of us is different as individuals.

Don't Speak in Doubt

Also, never speak in doubt. If you are not sure of what the Lord has given to you, and if you have the slightest doubt, sit down and shut up or you are going to make a fool out of yourself.

You are going to stand up and speak the biggest load of garbage. Know that what you have received is from the Lord. When you get that knot in your stomach and those butterflies the Lord is saying, "Go and speak."

"Oh Lord, only three words? All you've given me is a vision. I don't even know what it means."

That is different. But when you are not sure and say, "Umm, I don't know," then don't speak. Rather err on the side of keeping quiet, because if you stand up and speak in doubt you are going to make a fool out of yourself and nobody is going to listen to you the next time round. They will say, "The last time he stood up he spoke garbage."

You may have even had a really good word that is true, but the timing is wrong and if you feel this, "Umm, I don't know," then rather sit down. Don't share it. Keep quiet. The time may not be right. The person may not be ready. Whatever the situation is, never speak if you have any doubt in your heart. I promise that the Lord will not curse you! If you have missed it by sitting down, then He is well able to raise up another to share.

He is also well able to give you another word for next time. So do not feel pressured, but simply follow what you feel in your spirit.

Be Who God Made You

This one may make you laugh, but do not try to be a teacher if you are a prophet. I had someone who wrote to me with some teachings. She is a prophet – a really good one.

I received these teachings in the mail with about ten scriptures and a load of verbal intellect all expressed through technical words and high language. It was so deep that nobody could grasp what she was saying.

Why was this? Did it mean she didn't have a ministry? No, it meant that she was trying to be a teacher when really she was a prophet. She dug into her concordance and pulled out a whole lot of scriptures on her little hobbyhorse, and now she was going to teach it.

You couldn't even get through the first two paragraphs and you were bored!

So don't stand up behind a pulpit or stand up to share with somebody with a whole lot of scriptures and try to be a teacher when you are prophet.

Be who you are. Be who God has called you to be. A teacher might look cleverer and a prophet may look all fluffy and flying by the wind all the time, but that is what God has made you to be. Just be who He has called you to be. Don't try and be anything else.

Don't Impose Your Ministry

Next, don't impose your ministry on others. We have a lot of needy prophets running around out there that just can't wait to minister. They see somebody and think, "Ooh, she's got a need! I can see she's got one. Wait till I get to her. I'm going to minister to her. Wait till I'm finished with her. She's going to be thrilled!"

No, she will not be thrilled. She didn't want anybody running up to her, laying hands on her and prophesying to her. Some people do not like it like that. Do not impose your ministry on other people.

Do's & Don'ts of Prophetic Presentation

Because you have such a great need to minister don't run up to them and fall over your feet to give them a prophetic word if they didn't ask for it. Don't go laying your hands on anybody and praying for them when they didn't ask for it, and don't tell them what the Lord is saying if they didn't ask.

You say, "The problem with you is you need to do this, this and this. The Lord is telling you to do this, that and the next thing."

They say, "Well, I don't care! I never asked you."

The Lord Jesus does not impose Himself on us. We should not impose ourselves on others. And sometimes it is difficult because you see that there are people with needs. You look at them and you can see the need.

You know they need to hear from God. You know that you have what they need, but don't go imposing it on them if they didn't ask for it, because you are wasting your time. You might actually ruin and destroy something the Lord had been doing to prepare their hearts.

By going and forcing your ministry on them you are actually destroying their future ministry opportunities.

Skip the Bible Bashing

You see much of this in evangelism as well. You have the evangelist who will come in and bash a poor little co-worker and impose on him all the time. That is why

Christians came to be known as Bible bashers. They would bash people over their heads with a Bible and impose on them. They don't want ministry, so don't offer it. That is our rule. If somebody does not ask for prayer, we don't give it.

We will say, "I see this" and we will leave it there. If they receive it and say, "Will you pray for me?" we will pray. If they do not ask however we will not pray, because their hearts may not be ready to receive and you are wasting your time.

And worse, you will actually get a backlash. Whatever they are going through, if you minister prematurely when they didn't ask for it, they are going to reject your ministry and you will get the attack that has been on them. So don't go running into the war unarmed. Make sure that you are prepared.

Don't Dominate

Don't dominate the meeting. If you are preaching you can dominate the meeting and everyone has to listen, but generally don't do it. Prophets love the sounds of their own voices sometimes. Have you noticed that? They can talk and talk for hours. Eventually you are saying, "I wish he would shut up!" Been there! Done that!

Amongst all the don'ts, I am sure you are flinching as much as I am. There is this consolation though... you are not alone in your failures. Anyone with a prophetic call has tripped over one or more of these mistakes. The secret here is not to let it discourage you, but to inspire you to greatness!

So to get back to our point, don't dominate the meeting. There may be others that the Lord wants to use. Don't stand up and think that because you are the best at it, that you are the only one for the job.

Give other people a chance. Give them place to grow. Don't go in and dominate and don't always be the one to bring the prophetic word. Don't always jump in there all the time, especially if you are mature. If you are immature it is different, then get out there and exercise your ministry. But if you are mature in the gifts and you are comfortable in it, sometimes it is good to sit down and give somebody else a chance.

Let them grow and get to the place that you have come to. It doesn't mean that because the Lord always uses you to bring prophetic words that there is not somebody else that He wants to use.

If you just sit down and be quiet, you might be surprised at who He raises up to speak next. You might just be surprised to see who had a prophetic ministry brewing there all along, but never had the chance to stand up and speak, because you jumped up before them. Wait on the Lord. Be still. Let Him move on others and you will start seeing other ministries coming forth.

Don't Look for Feedback

Never keep looking at a person for feedback. This is a big one. When you are giving somebody personal direction, don't look at them directly and say, "The Lord has called you to be a teacher, and you're going to teach youth?" and you look at them for confirmation. They don't respond so you say, "You're going to teach adults," and the person confirms it.

If you do this, you are prophesying out of your mind. Don't look at them for feedback and stare them down. Not only is it intimidating, but you are going to be tempted to start thinking in your mind. You are going to say something and then go, "No, that's not what I meant. I meant...," until you get the recognition from them and say, "Yes, that's what God has called you to do!"

You are not prophesying. You are speaking out of your head. Just speak what God tells you to speak. If we prophesy over somebody you will notice that we do it with our eyes closed. This is for the simple reason that I don't want to see what reactions I am getting.

I am hearing from the Lord. A lot of the time the Lord speaks to me in visions. When I am prophesying I see visions and I speak what I see, so if I am looking at you all the time and concentrating on every feature and body movement I am not going to hear what God is saying.

Keep quiet for a minute, close your eyes and see what He has to say for the person. Then while you have your eyes closed and you are meditating in the Spirit, it will start flowing out. Then it doesn't matter what they look like or what they are doing. You are going to see change.

Dos of Presenting Prophecy

So how did you compare? Have you done any of those things? I have probably done most of them so don't worry about it. There are, however, some do's, and maybe you can tick off some of these as well and feel a little bit better about yourself.

Represent Jesus

Speak loudly and clearly. I have covered this a bit already. Speak with boldness. You are representing the King of Kings here. You are not speaking on behalf of yourself.

This isn't Colette Toach that is speaking. This is Jesus. When I speak the Word of God to you it isn't me, it is the Lord speaking to you. You know, if I am representing Christ I had better look like I'm representing Him.

Would Christ stand up and mumble and fumble and trip over His feet? No He wouldn't. He would speak directly. You are representing the King of Kings, so look like you are representing the King of Kings.

You know you get an impression of somebody by the person who represents them. People get an impression of my husband by the way I represent him. If I meet you for the first time I am representing the kind of husband I have, and you get an image in your mind of what he is like by what I am.

It is the same with the Lord. People get an impression of God by the way you represent Him. How are you representing Him, because whenever you stand up to speak, however you stand up to speak, they are getting an impression of what God is like?

So make sure you are representing Him according to his stature. He is a King – the greatest King. Look like you are representing the greatest King, because it is a tremendous honor to stand and speak for the King. Stand up and look like you are speaking for the King, because you are. It is what God has given you. It is what you are called to do.

Be neat and watch your physical appearance. Take care of yourself. Give something that they want to look at. Nobody wants to look at somebody whose appearance is shabby.

They want to look at somebody who is dressed well, is neat and tidy and has a good presentation. I am not saying go overboard on the externals and on works, but be presentable to God's people because it is a sign of respect to both the Lord and the Church.

If you had a meeting with the president of the United States, I doubt very much that you would show up with your dirty shirt from last week, accentuated by your frayed flip-flops! No, you would wear your best.

How much more when we stand and represent the King? That is why we have set a good standard in our ministry. When I make an effort to dress appropriately, I am showing you respect. I am saying, "You are important enough for me to make an effort with my appearance."

Zeal and Anointing

Share with zeal and anointing. Share with the same excitement that is within you. You know there is something about being around somebody who is excitable. You find yourself being drawn in to them. You are around somebody who is excited about something.

They are talking and they are excited. Their face is beaming, and you want to get in on the action! You want to be part of that. Share with that same zeal. Share with fire and don't hold back. Don't try and be so spiritual that you bore them to sleep.

Speak with that zeal and passion that is within you, because when you speak with that zeal people want to listen to you. They will open their hearts wide and say, "I want that!"

Speak with fire. Never stand up to speak unless you have fire. Speak with the real passion that is within you. I know this is difficult for those who are unemotional, so don't try and put on the emotion.

Just think, "How do I feel when I think on this? What really burns in me?" Then speak with that burning. Even the most unemotional person can have emotion when they are speaking about something that excites them. Their eyes will sparkle. Their face will light up, and it makes the world of difference. It can also make or break a prophetic word.

The word may be of God, but if you don't share it with that excitement and true desire, people are not going to listen. They are not going to receive. If you stand up and mumble your prophetic word and hope everybody listens to you, forget it, you have lost them.

The word was thrown to the wind. It was there by the stones and the birds got it. It was in the thorns and it never bore fruit. It was not because of the word. The word was true, but because of the way you presented it, it was lost.

Be Simple

Share using simple language. There are some people that stand up and speak as though they have a dictionary inside their heads. You look at them and think, "Well I hope they understood what he was saying, because I don't have a clue."

Everybody is too embarrassed to say, "I didn't really understand what you said," so they all go, "Amen brother." However, inside you are thinking, "Oh Lord, I don't have a clue."

You are too embarrassed to say to the guy next to you, "What did he say?" because then you will look like an idiot, so everybody just pretends and says, "Yeah, great word! What did it mean?"

"I don't have a clue."

"It was a great word though."

Now you might sound intelligent and you may look intelligent, but if they didn't understand you, the word is not going to bear fruit, so don't use such high language.

Once again we have really had to learn this when speaking with people from different countries. I can't use colloquialism, euphemisms and puns and all the things that are common to my culture. I used them at first and I had some Americans thinking, "What is she talking about?" I would crack a joke that was really hilarious where I come from and I would look around and nobody was laughing.

"They're not laughing! Why aren't they laughing?"

It was because it was something that was familiar to my culture and something where if I had a group full of South Africans they would have doubled over laughing. The Americans didn't seem to share my sense of humor and it took me a while to get their sense of humor. It is different. The way they speak is different and their terminology is different.

I had to change the way I said things like, "It is not a serviette, it is a napkin," and that sort of thing. If I use the wrong terminology they don't know what I am talking about. And so use words that are simple and that everybody can relate to, so that especially if you are an international ministry everybody can grasp and receive from you. Especially if you are preaching as well, use simple language.

Keep Going

If you fumble, pick yourself up and get back on track. We all mess up. We all get tongue-tied, especially because we are talking so fast. I do it all the time. If it happens just stop, take a breath and carry on as though nothing happened.

Everybody will wait for you, but they won't wait for continual stumbling and fumbling. They get uncomfortable. If you are starting to fumble and get tongue-tied just stop, take a breath, get yourself together and carry on. It will make the world of difference and you would have saved face.

Pick yourself up and keep going. Don't stop and run away either. Just keep going. Get back on track. The Lord will forgive you. The people will forgive you, and nobody will remember next time.

Personal Matters

When you share a vision do not presume its interpretation. When I get a vision for somebody I share the vision with them. They might already have the interpretation.

God could have already been speaking to their hearts, so don't presume otherwise you will look a bit like a fool when you say, "The Lord is saying this," and they go, "Actually that vision makes sense, because the Lord gave me the same one a week ago." Simply share the vision and throw it out there. It may witness with their spirit and they might already have the interpretation.

So, share personal issues privately. We get revelation all the time. It is the way the Lord has made us as prophets, but you know when you get revelation of somebody's sins or hurts of the past, or private issues, don't blab it out in front of everybody.

It is embarrassing. They are not going to receive the word, because they will be too red-faced to even want to listen to you.

Take them aside and say, "When we were praying the Lord showed me this."

Share it with them privately and their hearts will be open to receive, and you will be a confirmation to them instead of an embarrassment to them.

Share in love through God's eyes. Sometimes you get this unsavory character coming for prayer and you think, "Oh yeah, I know what God's going to say. He's got sin. I'm going to give him both barrels and say it as it is down the line," because of an assessment that you have made.

You know, when you look through God's eyes and you look at them in love you see a whole different picture. This unsavory character who looks full of rebellion and full of nonsense might have the softest heart you ever saw.

But because you are looking at the externals you don't see the soft heart. When you come to speak and prophesy especially in personal ministry always look through the eyes of Christ. Don't look through your natural eyes, because your natural eyes will let you down every time.

Submit to Authority

Do submit to your local authority. Don't stand up in a local church that you know is against the gifts of the Spirit and speaking in tongues and then go off in tongues. Don't do it. I don't care if the word you got was from God.

Submit it to the authority first. If you know it is going to cut across the grain of what they teach, present the word to the authority. If they reject the word the blood of God's people is on their hands, but you delivered the word. You delivered the package.

However, you don't stand up in the sheepfold of another shepherd and send his flock scattering and running in seven directions. You don't have authority to do that. They are in his care. I don't just let anybody come into my house and tell my kids what to do. Heaven help any person that comes in and says to my children, "You must wear this. And you must do this and the next thing."

I say, "Hey, who do you think you are?"

However, if somebody comes to me and says, "I really feel that your daughter needs to do this," or, "I really feel that she needs to do that," I can then receive that word and relay it to my children. But I don't just have anybody coming into my house and causing a ruckus.

It is the same in the body of Christ. There is an order of doing things. Don't just go in and usurp the authority of the local elders, because you have a word from God.

Your word may be real, but because of the way you present it, you are actually going to cause confusion. If you want the people of God to hear it then their leadership must agree with it, because when the leadership agrees with it the sheep will look up to the leadership and they will also agree with it.

It works like this. You don't start from the bottom up. Start from the top down. If the pastor rejects the word, the blood of God's people is on his hands. You have delivered your word and you step back.

Then you pray and you intercede that that pastor receives revelation, but you do not stand up in church and deliver a word that you know is in complete disagreement with what the pastor has been preaching, and against what he has been telling the congregation.

You would be causing a division and actually bring more harm than good that way.

I know that it is so tempting when you see hurting people that need to hear this word. You can see that there are things that are wrong, but you are going to cause more confusion by speaking.

Speak to the leader. If he agrees then speak to the people. If he disagrees then you go to your prayer closet and pray. You intercede and speak into their lives from afar. You decree and speak to them from your closet, and that decree will bring change in their hearts if you cannot speak it to their faces.

Share in humility. Yes, be bold, but don't think you are so great that you are the greatest prophet that ever lived and they must hear the word you speak, because you are so wonderful. Be humble. It is not me that stands here. It is Christ. I represent Christ, but you know what? At the end of the day it is Him. It is His word, it is His authority. It is His anointing and His power.

Always Bring Change

In conclusion of this chapter, the presentation makes or breaks what you are going to share. Give the people of God something they want to hear. Give it to them in a way that they want to receive it.

Don't give it to them so that they run for the door. Don't be one of those prophets that you see in the Old Testament with a stick in their one hand and a club in the other, coming to bash God's people. They are going to run away from you.

You will be a John the Baptist type living in the Wilderness with your hair gone wild, eating locusts and wearing shabby clothes. That may have worked for John the Baptist, but he didn't live in the twenty-first century.

He was the last of the Old Testament prophets. You are not called to eat locusts. Thank the Lord you're not called to eat locusts and wild honey and you're not called to be a wild and crazy man!

You are called to represent the King with the indwelling of the Holy Spirit. Represent Him and leave God's people changed. That is always your goal. As a prophet, keep this in mind. Your end goal always is to bring change.

Once you have finished speaking say to yourself, "Did that word change anybody's life? Did that word change anybody's heart? Did it leave them with something to think about? Did it leave them with a seed in their hearts, or did it just go in one ear and out the other? Did they receive? Did I speak in such a way that they received?" because if they did not receive it they will not change.

Before you stand up and after you have finished, stand up and say, "Did I bring change?"

Even if you mess up on all those points; even if you looked a mess and you fumbled your words and spoke too softly but you brought change, this is the most important point. You will mess up. All of us will mess up, but the anointing cuts through all of that. You can mess up and the Holy Spirit will still empower your mess up and bring change, and that is the ultimate in presenting prophecy.

CHAPTER 08

Ministering to Others

Chapter 08 – Ministering to Others

Introduction – Learning When to Step Forward & When Back

When I was about thirteen years old, the school I went to, decided to teach us how to do some ballroom dancing. Now, I had never done any kind of dancing before, so this was my first experience with it.

I am short to make matters worse and it also just took me a while to get the hang of it – more than it took the other kids. I didn't know when to step forward and when to step back and I ended up stepping on my partner's feet more than anything else.

It was a good experience though and after a bit of practice I eventually started getting it right. Like I said though, being so short really didn't help because I had such tall partners who had such long legs. To keep up with them I often had to take close to two steps. It was a bit crazy.

As we have been talking about the prophetic ministry and especially as we get into the more practical parts of it, I realized that prophesying and functioning as a prophet is a bit like learning how to ballroom dance.

Even though you are led by the Holy Spirit, it takes a bit of skill. You have to learn when to step forward and when to sit down. Now, for most prophets, I think the main problem is learning when to shut up more than when to speak.

You are probably the one jumping ahead too quickly and stepping on your partner's feet leaving them howling in pain. That is what most prophets seem to do. The poor pastor gets up to say something and before you know it the prophet jumps in there stepping on his feet saying, "This is the way it should be done!"

The prophet does this, only to realize that this was one of those times when he needed to step back instead of forward. This is what I would like to look at in this chapter.

God's Perfect Timing

People get this crazy idea that if you get a prophetic revelation it means you must share it. It means that if God gave you a revelation that now is the time to jump up and to tell the whole world. However, it is not like that!

Just because you receive revelation or just because you have the answers, doesn't mean that the whole world is ready to hear it. This is most certainly something we have even experienced in our ministry.

I mean, there were times when the Lord gave us a word and a direction and we thought now is the time, but the Lord said, "Now is NOT the time. My timing is different. "

I think about Moses and how he grew up in Pharaoh's household. The Word says that when Stephen gave his testimony that Moses knew that he was an Israelite and refused to be part of Pharaoh's household any longer.

After that you see how he steps in there trying to save the Israelites. He steps in and kills the slave driver. You really get the impression that Moses knew that he was called for a purpose. However, it wasn't time yet.

Right through the Scriptures we see revelations and promises of the Lord and they didn't come to pass until many years later. Why is that? It is because it wasn't time. However, when the time was right, it exploded.

You will experience the same thing in your prophetic walk. You have to learn how to dance this dance. You can't just go around and spin in circles as though you are running on your own.

This is a dance with the Holy Spirit and so there are times when you need to step forward and times when you need to step back. There are times when you do need to stand up and speak that word in the right time with authority. Then you will see things happen. However, oftentimes you need to just step back and wait.

The perfect word in the right time is truly like a double-edged sword. It is like a dynamite stick.

However, if you run ahead just sharing all your revelations then it's like a hand grenade without a pin.

It's like a dud. You need to have the two together. It has to be in the right time. You have to pull the pin at the right time and then also throw it at the right time.

You can't just go around throwing hand grenades everywhere. You have to do the right thing at the right time to bring the most impact.

Learn to Be Sensitive to the Spirit

Now this does take a little bit of skill. It will involve you having a bit of other-orientation and noticing other people. You know, I think sometimes we get so wound up on what we feel and what we think God is saying that we don't stop often enough to listen to people.

If you would just stop to listen to them and hear what they are really saying, you would get the revelation as well of when to step forward and when to step back. You have to learn to be sensitive to the spirit. Just because God has given you a revelation, doesn't mean that you have to share it right now.

In fact, I have seen that in my own personal experience. I have come to see that the revelation that God gives comes in stages. Consider Moses who went up the mountain again and again. He didn't receive the full picture right at the beginning. Not even David got the full picture of what God wanted him to do right at the beginning. It took some time.

It is a progress. You know, David got the whole pattern for the temple, but Solomon only built it years later. It was only years later that the time was right for this thing to be established.

So you need to learn some sensitivity. As a prophet especially if you flow in the gifts, you are going to get revelation. The Lord will share things with you. Certainly, as you go through all of our teachings you will learn the principles.

And so you will start to understand what's wrong with people without necessarily receiving revelation. Just from knowing the teachings you will know when somebody shows a need for acceptance and when somebody has a curse in their lives. You will also identify when someone is in bondage.

When you see these things so clearly you want to jump in and help. You want to get in there and get this dance together and make it happen.

Unless the other person is ready to receive what you have to say though, your word will fall on that dry, horrible ground and the birds will come and eat it up!

You may not always get good responses. Perhaps that is something you have experienced in times past… you end up jumping in there and sharing your five cents worth only to find out it wasn't worth anything to anyone else.

You ended up getting kicked out of your church or something. Let's just say you weren't the big favorite after that, were you? You opened your big mouth.

The prophet clearly is a pendulum swinger. You go from one extreme to the other, but it doesn't mean that you have to stay there. There comes a time, when you have to learn to be sensitive to the Holy Spirit.

So just because you see that there are things that are wrong in the Church, just because you see somebody is in bondage, doesn't mean that you should be jumping in and giving your opinion.

As I said, Moses thought he would get in there and hit the slave driver but killed him. What happened in the end? Did the Israelites say, "Oh, thank you Moses, you are the best. I can't wait for you to be our deliverer"? That's not what they said, is it?

When Moses tried to settle a quarrel between two Israelites just a little while later, they told him, "So what are you going to do? Are you going to kill us just like you killed that other guy?"

They had no respect for him. They didn't think that he was the best!

Perhaps you have been experiencing this in your ministry as well. You can't understand why people are just not receiving what you have to say.

Let's say you go to your pastor with good intentions and you say, "Look, these are the problems I see at the church and this is what I feel God is saying", and then you can't understand why you are getting preached at from the pulpit!

Was it the pastor's fault, or was it perhaps because you jumped in when you should have been stepping back and waiting for the wisdom and timing of the Lord?

This is a lesson I want you to learn right at the beginning of your prophetic walk. Learn the right timing. Certainly when you learn to mentor people you will come to realize that there is a right time to give the chisel and there is a right time to encourage. There is a right time and season for everything. Just like the Scriptures say, there is a time to be born and a time to die, a time to reap and a time to sow.

God has a perfect time. Just because He has revealed something to you that He needs you to share, doesn't mean that now you have to blab it out. Once you receive the revelation it is time for you to ask the Lord and say, "Okay, when do you want me to share it?"

If you do it that way you will do it in wisdom. When you share that word and the Lord has opened the way it will always go smoothly. However, if you try and push the door open, if you try and force your way in, you will upset the whole dance. Everybody will be upset with you. You will be the one upsetting the whole big group there with their nice little flow.

We prophets tend to just jump up because we can see the glory hallelujah. You think, "Can't the rest of them see it?" Actually, no they can't.

It was the same with the children of Israel. They didn't see it either when Moses jumped in there. It took them another 40 years to be ready. Then, when they were ready God rose up Moses and told him, "Okay Moses - now it's time for you to go back!"

The Revelation is Not Necessarily Wrong – It's Just the Timing

You see, it doesn't mean that the revelation you got was necessarily wrong! Think about times when you tried to share with somebody and gave them counsel but they rejected it. Does this mean that you missed it?

Not necessarily. Your revelation may have been spot on but perhaps that person was just not ready yet to receive what you had to say!

Just like Moses saw that Israelite in bondage, so do you see people who are bound all the time. So you want to jump in and say, "Hey, do you know that you are bound? Do you see that satan is binding you here? Do you know that you can break free? Do you know that this is a curse and if you just let go of this bitterness you can rise up?"

You see the problem – you are a prophet. It is one of those things you can do. You notice things! However, just because you notice things, doesn't give you a license to jump in and share them with others. Do it in God's perfect timing.

Consider the Lord Jesus when He walked this earth. He had so many parables to share. Did you know though that He didn't share everything with everyone? In fact, the Scripture says that He committed to no man. He even said to His disciples, "It's to you that I have revealed these things, not to everybody."

He would sit with them and share the parables and the explanations. Why didn't He just give it to everybody?

They weren't ready to receive everything He had to say. The disciples on the other hand were ready. And so He shared with them. Even with them though, did you notice how much he kept for the very end?

He had been with them for years but He waited till the Passover to make it clear to them that He was going to die and be resurrected. They didn't even understand that at the time yet. Even at the final supper they didn't fully understand and grasp it. It took some time and some death.

When He was crucified and they were scattered and had gone through the death, they were suddenly ready to hear the truth and understood the real purpose of why Jesus came.

He still in those three years couldn't share with them the full concept of what the Messiah had come to do! It wasn't to come and set the Roman Jews free from their bondage, it was to come and set us free from our sin!

Also consider the Gentiles and them being brought into the body of Christ. They weren't ready to receive that. Peter only received that later! It came in stages. They weren't ready for it.

Wait for the Body of Christ to Be Ready

It is the same in the body of Christ today. They are not ready for all the revelations. Jesus had all the revelations. He knew what was going to happen. He knew that He was going to die.

He didn't go around though blabbing it out all the time. You see, there is a right word for the right time. This will take some sensitivity on your part to really stop and sense the spirit.

You will learn how to use your spiritual Urim and Thummim so you can understand when it's time to speak and when it is time to remain quiet.

If you feel pushed and feel that you have to share this word, it is a very good reason not to. In fact, that always used to be a standard when I was going through my prophetic training. If I felt compelled to do anything, I would wait a day.

If by the next day, I still felt that desire in me then I would go ahead. If I didn't, then I knew it was just the enemy pushing me.

You know, people think that getting into deception means that you are getting a false revelation from satan. Whereas this is also valid, you will come to find out that you will fail more often in allowing satan to push you beyond what God intended. This will happen more often than you receiving demonic revelation.

He will push you with the things you are receiving and say, "You have to share it now. You have to go to that pastor and let them know."

Perhaps the revelation you got was even genuine. However, the pushiness causes you to go beyond what God intended and so you end sharing in the wrong timing. This in turn makes you face rejection (which is the middle name of the prophet) and you are back in the vicious circle.

So let me do you a favor and save you from this rejection by learning to do things in God's time. This is probably the greatest lesson you will ever learn in ministry in general, not even just in the prophetic. Learn when to hold back. When you feel unsure in your spirit, listen to it. Listen to what's inside of you.

Instead of letting your mind get in the way all the time, listen to your spirit. The Holy Spirit will never pressure you. He will lead you, but He will not pressure you. Then when you step out, you will feel the anointing and it will flow.

If you are stepping out and it is always going wrong, you need to check your motivations. Perhaps this time wait on the Lord a little. Granted, not every word you give is always going to be well received. When the Lord opens the way though, it's well received a lot more often than when you are pushy.

So... When is the Time to Get Involved?

I have taught you much on when to step back and wait. So now, let's look at when it is time for you to step forward. It is the opposite extreme that I don't see too often with prophets.

You know, the best time to get involved with the person is to wait for the open door. People will always give you the opportunity.

Let's say for example, the Lord has given you a revelation and you feel that the Lord is about to lead somebody you know into a new direction. You may see that the Lord has a new door for them. You happen to bump into them or see them at the next meeting and you are dying to share what you have received...

So what are you going to do? Walk up to them and share what God says? I don't suggest doing that until you are in prophetic office and are really sure of the voice of God.

What you can do though is go to this person, listen to them and just wait. You listen to what they are saying and you wait for the Lord to open the door.

When He opens the door then it is time to jump in. You know what the problem is though? The problem is that you are not listening! You are not looking at people and are not hearing what they are not saying; never mind what they are saying.

You don't hear anything at all. You are just set on your revelation. You feel that you must say this and must do that… Instead of just saying, "Okay Lord, you have given me a revelation, please open the door! "

If the Lord has given you something to share, then put it into His hands. It is His word and not yours!

If He gave you the word in the first place, then He will surely open the door for you to share it also.

Don't Pounce on People

Say you are meeting with this person and you are talking and you know the Lord has given you this word to share. What are you going to do? Pounce on them after the meeting and say, "God says…"?

And you can't understand why they are running out the back door as fast as they can and don't talk to you again….

Nobody likes to be pounced on. It is kind of like a salesman trying to sell you. You know those that hang out outside the stores sometimes and you go past them and they grab you and say, "Can I interest you in this?" Oh, I hate it!

I like it to be able to go into the store, get what I want and make the choice. Then if the salesman is there, I appreciate it. I can ask him a question if need be. If somebody grabs me while I am on my merry way though, I don't like it.

Unfortunately, prophets do the body of Christ that way. They are grabbing people in the street... You know, just chill out and let them come to you. Let them come ready to receive.

When the Lord is in control then you can be sure that the conversation will turn. They will start mentioning something that will be right in line with what God showed you and then it's your time to step in.

Then you can say, "You know, the Lord actually showed me something the other day when I was praying for you."

You see, they are already open to receive because they brought it up in the first place. Therefore, their hearts will be wide open and ready to receive.

Like I said though, you know what the main problem is? It's not your revelation or even the person not being ready to receive. It is that you don't know how to listen to people. You are not noticing them. You are not really listening to what they are saying. This is really one of the most important things!

This project is foundational for any kind of ministry and it will transform your entire approach to ministry. I guarantee it. You will go from one level to the next.

I don't even care if you are new to ministry or have been in it for 20 years, when you learn these simple principles, you will be the kind of person that everybody will come to receive from.

They won't feel threatened. They will feel comfortable around you. In fact, they might be so much at ease that you might have to schedule some appointments. You will get very busy.

What Are You Going to Do? GET INVOLVED!

So how do you know when you need to step in with people? Well, learn to listen for the hints.

You say to somebody for instance, "Hey, how are you doing today?"

In response they say, "You know, yeah… we are good. We are great!"

Now you have a choice to make. You can either say leave it at that and reply with a smile or press on.

Especially in our politically correct society today everything is so superficial. You go to the store and you hear, "Did you find everything okay? Ah, that's nice… everything is fine!" Nobody wants to hear that you are doing horribly!

Nobody wants to hear that you have had the worst week ever. They just want to hear the "good, good, everything is fine" sort of thing!

Are you really prepared to get involved with people or do you just want to give them all the prophetic words and show them how great you are?

Prophetic ministry, in fact, any ministry, is real work and so it takes real effort. It takes getting involved with real people. Do you want some practical experience in ministry? Then open your eyes, because it is all around you.

There are people with needs all around you, starting with your spouse, your kids, your friends and family, even your associates. You name it!

All you need to do now is learn to listen. You want God to use you. You want Him to give you an outlet for ministry and here He is busy trying and you don't see it. Just open your eyes around you, there are people with needs everywhere.

If you took the time to listen to what people are saying and would just get involved in their lives in a good way, the Lord will give you revelation as well as the tools you need to minister to them.

So you want the word of knowledge or wisdom… for what? Just so you can say you have it? If you have an other-orientation, if you have a heart for people, God will give you what you need.

Just love people and God will give you what you need to love them with.

If you just want to heal and restore them and be there for them, the gifts will flow. I promise you! The gifts will come naturally to you in fact.

CHAPTER 09

Master Other-Orientation

Chapter 09 – Master Other-Orientation

People are struggling all the time, just learn to notice it! Listen to the hints and the things they don't say. People drop hints all the time in a conversation. Let's be honest, you know they do and even pick it up. You have just been trained to shut it out. It's not politically correct to get involved.

Listen to the Hints

Let's just say you are in a conversation with somebody you met for the first time. You are walking along and you are getting to know each other. You talk about where you are from and so on and so forth. Then the question of marriage comes up. They ask you if you are married and you share and then you throw the question back at them and they say, "Oh, my husband died last year."

You have a choice to make right here. You can ignore that statement and the fact that they even brought it up, or you can choose to get involved and take that step forward. When you take that step forward, ministry can follow.

You could for example turn to her and say, "Man, that's really tough. What happened? Tell me about it." Then she can respond by sharing everything with you or she can cut you off and change the topic.

If that happens, then you know that she doesn't want to go there. At that point you are not going to force ministry on her.

You see, it is like a dance! She steps forward by asking the marriage question, you step forward by asking the question of what happened. Then you step back and wait for her to make the next move. Will she share with you what happened or will she change the conversation?

Let's say she shares everything that happened with you. Let me tell you something - you are probably one of the first people that asked. Honestly, nobody knows what to do with somebody who has lost a loved one.

Nobody knows how to really show love in this situation. Let me give you a hint right now. You just need to care. You don't even have to have the answers, have great revelation or be a counselor. You just need to love them and listen.

People really don't take time for that and so this in itself is already one of the most incredible ministries. Just listen and let her share her story with you of how he died and what happened.

So now that she has shared her story, what are you going to do next?

You will say to her, "And how are you handling it now? How has it been for you? Have you got over it?" You can simply ask her how she is doing with it. Then she will have a choice again. She might share with you and let you know that she feels really lonely and misses him. She may even cry.

That is when you step in and minister and let her know that the Lord Jesus is always there with her. You can say, "He has not forsaken you and He has got something better for you."

Just as you step out and do that, you will start receiving visions, you will get words of wisdom, and you will start getting revelation. You will feel the anointing in a way that you have never felt it in your life, because this is real life ministry!

That is prophetic ministry 101. It is not when you get up on Sunday and give your big prophetic word that nobody ever remembers anyway. However, when you minister to somebody with a real problem and a real hurt, you bring change to their life. You bring Christ to them. Now you are doing prophetic ministry.

Master the Skill

Until you have mastered this skill of other-orientation, you haven't even begun to walk in prophetic ministry never mind office.

You see, you can make your ministry available, but then it is for people to decide if they want it or not.

Coming back to the illustration of the salesman, I like the kind that let me know that he is there for me if I need any help. I can handle that. However, the ones that try to push their views down your throat are a bit more difficult to handle.

There is nothing worse than having a nice dinner with your family and the telephone rings and the guy keeps going on and on about what and why you should buy from him. It drives you nuts, doesn't it?

Well, aren't you doing the body of Christ that way with your revelations?

Yet when there is somebody with a real problem, you are not doing anything about it. Perhaps your neighbor is going through a crisis. Their teenage daughter just fell pregnant. What are you doing with a situation like this?

Are you gossiping like the rest of the neighborhood or are you knocking on their door saying, "Hey, I heard what happened. How are you guys holding up? Is there anything I can do for you?" Are you approaching them even if it means to just sit there and listen…?

When you hear people's stories and see the things they are going through and take your eyes off yourself for five minutes you can't help but feel the compassion.

You know, right next door to you there are people being abused, beaten and hurt. They are facing financial crises, physical attacks, they get sick…Just look around you and get involved.

Say your husband gets home from work and he's got that look on his face again. What are you going to say? "Baby, what happened today? You look stressed!"

Then he offloads on you. You know, that's good! Take the time to listen to him. What if you have children, especially teenagers, are you really listening to them or are you just phasing out what you don't want to hear and only care about the stuff you want to hear…?

When they come home and look a bit down, what do you say? "What happened?"

"Well, I had a conflict with this person and this friend…" or don't they ever get to share that stuff with you because you just don't listen?

It really takes so little of our time and if you can develop this skill, you will be a professional dancer in no time at all.

Three Steps for Ministering to Others

Let me take you through three very simple steps to offering your ministry to anyone at any time.

1. Listen to what people are saying (or not saying).
2. Offer them what you have.
3. Do not proceed until they are open to receive.

Get involved. Listen to what they have to say and let them know that you can help, but wait for their approval. Either they will come up with an excuse to leave the conversation or they will share more with you.

If you follow these three simple steps every time you step out to minister, you will be successful. As a side note, it is obvious what people say to you and what they are going through but it's really what they are not saying that often shouts the loudest.

Let's say you have a co-worker and he is always speaking about his kids. He talks about all the plans he has for the future, but he never tells you about his wife. What does that tell you? You know he has been married for a while, but he keeps on talking about everything but her.

It tells you that this is a sore point. So what are you going to do about it? You could ignore it or you could say, "Hey, how is your wife doing?" or, "Hey, aren't you married? How long have you been married for?"

Then you can see if he is prepared to talk about it or not. He may say, "Ah yeah, she is okay. We haven't seen each other for a while, because of this and that."

You know clearly that there is a problem there when he shares something like this. You could say, "Oh wow that sounds tough! How are you handling that?"

Get involved! The Holy Spirit will open your eyes. The minute you commit yourself to this the Holy Spirit will open your eyes in a way that you cannot begin to imagine.

So are you ready for it? Are you ready to transform and be transformed into the fullness of what God has for you?

I want you to take this "other-orientation" project seriously. This is foundational for every single ministry you will ever do whether it is prophetic or anything else. The other-orientation stands as one of the key points for a successful ministry and it is really what sets one person apart from the other.

As a bit of a practical conclusion of this chapter, I encourage you to do the following over the course of a week.

The Other-Orientation Project

1. Make a list of people you see on a regular basis (like your family, friends, co-workers).
    a. Make a list of the things they share with you. Make yourself available to minister to them.
    b. Write down some of the things they shared that were a cry for help.
    c. Make yourself available to them as they cry for help.
    d. Document if they accepted it or not.
    e. What was the general outcome of this?

You may find this a bit challenging, but as you do it you will grow. Make it your goal to get involved and to really listen to people.

Your ministry is about to take off in a way that you cannot imagine. Go into the Church and take it by storm!

About the Author

Born in Bulawayo, Zimbabwe and raised in South Africa, Colette had a zeal to serve the Lord from a young age. Coming from a long line of Christian leaders and having grown up as a pastor's kid she is no stranger to the realities of ministry. Despite having to endure many hardships such as her parent's divorce, rejection, and poverty, she continues to follow after the Lord passionately. Overcoming these obstacles early in her life has built a foundation of compassion and desire to help others gain victory in their lives.

Since then, the Lord has led Colette, with her husband Craig Toach, to establish *Apostolic Movement International,* a ministry to train and minister to Christian leaders all over the world, where they share all the wisdom that the Lord has given them through each and every time they chose to walk through the refining fire in their personal lives, as well as in ministry.

In addition, Colette is a fantastic cook, an amazing mom to not only her 4 natural children, but to her numerous spiritual children all over the world. Colette is also a renowned author, mentor, trainer and a woman that has great taste in shoes! The scripture to "be all things to all men" definitely applies here, and the Lord keeps adding to that list of things each and every day.

How does she do it all? Experience through every book and teaching the life of an apostle firsthand, and get the insight into how the call of God can make every aspect of your life an incredible adventure.

Read more at www.colette-toach.com

Connect with Colette Toach on Facebook!
www.facebook.com/ColetteToach

Check Colette out on Amazon.com at:
www.amazon.com/author/colettetoach

Recommendations by the Author

Note: All reference of AMI refers to Apostolic Movement International.

If you enjoyed this book, we know you will love the following on the prophetic.

I'm Not Crazy - I'm a Prophet

By Colette Toach

It It takes a prophet to know a prophet!

Only when you have been scorched yourself with this ministry, can you appreciate the gold hidden in this book.

You do not have to follow in the footsteps of others before you take the wealth of this book and rise above the pit falls.

That is why Colette Toach can take the prophetic and dish it out in its truth and cover the subjects included in this book.

So are you Crazy? Maybe a little, but this book will help you to be the true prophet that God has called you to be!

Colette Toach

Practical Prophetic Ministry

By Colette Toach

Wouldn't it be incredible if someone could have walked you through your prophetic calling and pointed out all the potholes before you fell into them?

Unfolded step by step, you will have someone along the way telling you what to avoid, what to embrace and most importantly... what to do next along your prophetic journey.

Prophetic Essentials

Book 1 of the Prophetic Field Guide Series

By Colette Toach

In this book, you will find out that the call of the prophet goes far deeper than the functions and duties that the prophet fulfills. Anyone flowing in prophetic ministry can carry out tasks similar to the prophet.

If it burns in you to pay any price that is necessary and to stand up and break down the barriers between the Lord Jesus and His Bride, then my friend, you have picked up the right tool that will confirm the fire in your belly and the call of God on your life.

Prophetic Functions

Book 2 of the Prophetic Field Guide Series

By Colette Toach

There is so much more to the prophet than standing up in church and prophesying.

Laid out beautifully so that you can understand and relate, Colette shares from her own personal experiences. Be prepared to live and experience the Lord like never before. This is not fiction... this is your training guide to the prophetic.

Prophetic Anointing

Book 3 of the Prophetic Field Guide Series

By Colette Toach

God has promised you a visit to the throne room! This is your summons from Almighty God. It is time for you to experience Him face-to-face and heart-to-heart.

Get ready for the meeting of a lifetime. The veils that have hindered the anointing in your life are going to be ripped away, and you are going to shine with His glory in every area of your life.

A.M.I. Prophetic School

www.prophetic-school.com

Whether you are just starting out or have been along the way for some time, we all have questions.

Who better to answer them than another prophet!

With over 18 years of experience, the A.M.I. Prophetic School is the leader in the prophetic realm.

From dedicated lecturers to live streaming and graduation, the A.M.I. Prophetic School is your home away from home.

What Our Prophetic Training Accomplishes

Our extensive training is a full two-year curriculum that will:

1. Identify and confirm your prophetic call
2. Effectively train you to flow in all the gifts of the Spirit
3. Fulfill your purpose as a prophet in the local church
4. Take your hand through the prophetic training process
5. Specialist training in spiritual warfare
6. Arm you for intercession and decree
7. Minister in praise and worship
8. Achieve prophetic maturity

Contact Information

To check out our wide selection of materials, go to: www.ami-bookshop.com

Do you have any questions about any products?

Contact us at: +1 (760) 466 - 7679
(8am to 5pm California Time, Weekdays Only)

E-mail Address: admin@ami-bookshop.com

Postal Address:

>A.M.I.
>5663 Balboa Ave #416
>San Diego, CA 92111, USA

Facebook Page:
http://www.facebook.com/ApostolicMovementInternational

YouTube Page:
https://www.youtube.com/c/ApostolicMovementInternational

Twitter Page: https://twitter.com/apmoveint

Amazon.com Page: www.amazon.com/author/colettetoach

AMI Bookshop – It's not Just Knowledge, It's **Living Knowledge**

www.ingramcontent.com/pod-product-compliance
Lightning Source LLC
Chambersburg PA
CBHW070453100426
42743CB00010B/1596